# PHOTOGRAPHING AMBIGUITY

*Photographing Ambiguity* examines photography as a metaphor for technological culture, arguing that a relational exploration of the medium can shed light on the dominant ideological tendencies of our time. The book advocates for photographic practices that emphasize ambiguity, suggesting that this approach fosters more conscientious, ecological, and creative relationships within the technological ecosystem of contemporary life.

Ted Hiebert critiques the notion that images should primarily serve to verify or document the external world. He contends that these quantifiable perspectives, while rooted in historical trends towards technology and data, have become so pervasive that they represent a dominant ideological bias in the twenty-first century. In response to this data-driven consciousness, the book presents a series of exercises designed to cultivate an embodied experience with digital living – not in opposition to the flood of images but within it. Ultimately, *Photographing Ambiguity* encourages readers to understand photographs not as benchmarks of reality but as ambiguous constructions of our present and future imaginaries.

(Digital Futures)

TED HIEBERT is a professor and chair of the School of Image Arts at Toronto Metropolitan University.

# DIGITAL FUTURES

*Series Editor: ARTHUR KROKER, University of Victoria*

Digital Futures is a series of critical examinations of technological development and the transformation of contemporary society by technology. The concerns of the series are framed by the broader traditions of literature, humanities, politics, and the arts. Focusing on the ethical, political, and cultural implications of emergent technologies, the series looks at the future of technology through the "digital eye" of the writer, new media artist, political theorist, social thinker, cultural historian, and humanities scholar. The series invites contributions to understanding the political and cultural context of contemporary technology and encourages ongoing creative conversations on the destiny of the wired world in all of its utopian promise and real perils.

## Editorial Advisory Board

David Cook, University of Toronto
Ronald Deibert, University of Toronto
Christopher Dewdney, York University
Sara Diamond, Ontario College of Art & Design University
Ricardo Dominguez, University of California, San Diego
nichola feldman-kiss, Toronto, ON/Pouch Cove, NL
Renate Ferro, Cornell University
Anita Girvan, UBC, Okanagan Campus
Johnny Golding, Royal College of Art, London
Ted Hiebert, Toronto Metropolitan University
Jessica Kolopenuk, University of Alberta
Pierre Lévy, University of Ottawa
Jackson Leween, 2bears, Western University
Lev Manovich, Graduate Center, CUNY
Liam Mitchell, Trent University
Timothy Murray, Cornell University
Marcos Novak, University of California, Santa Barbara
Stephen Pfohl, Boston College
Avital Ronell, New York University
Jentery Sayers, University of Victoria
Allucquére Rosanne (Sandy) Stone, University of Texas, Austin

# PHOTOGRAPHING AMBIGUITY

TED HIEBERT

UNIVERSITY OF TORONTO PRESS
Toronto Buffalo London

© University of Toronto Press 2025
Toronto  Buffalo  London
utppublishing.com

ISBN 978-1-4875-0811-1 (cloth)    ISBN 978-1-4875-3758-6 (EPUB)
ISBN 978-1-4875-2567-5 (paper)    ISBN 978-1-4875-3757-9 (PDF)

Digital Futures

---

**Library and Archives Canada Cataloguing in Publication**

Title: Photographing ambiguity / Ted Hiebert.
Names: Hiebert, Ted, 1973–, author.
Series: Digital futures.
Description: Series statement: Digital futures | Includes bibliographical
references and index.
Identifiers: Canadiana (print) 20250147475 | Canadiana (ebook) 20250147505 |
ISBN 9781487508111 (cloth) | ISBN 9781487525675 (paper) |
ISBN 9781487537586 (EPUB) | ISBN 9781487537579 (PDF)
Subjects: LCSH: Photography – Social aspects. | LCSH: Digital images –
Social aspects. | LCSH: Technology – Social aspects.
Classification: LCC TR183 .H54 2025 | DDC 770.1 – dc23

---

Cover design: John Beadle
Cover image: Melissa Gueiros, *Smash*, photograph, 2017

We wish to acknowledge the land on which the University of Toronto Press
operates. This land is the traditional territory of the Wendat, the Anishnaabeg,
the Haudenosaunee, the Métis, and the Mississaugas of the Credit First Nation.

This book has been published with the help of a grant from the Federation
for the Humanities and Social Sciences, through the Awards to Scholarly
Publications Program, using funds provided by the Social Sciences and
Humanities Research Council of Canada.

University of Toronto Press acknowledges the financial support of the
Government of Canada, the Canada Council for the Arts, and the Ontario Arts
Council, an agency of the Government of Ontario, for its publishing activities.

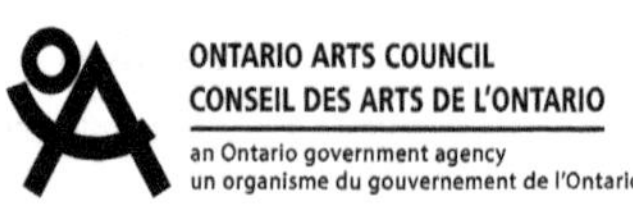

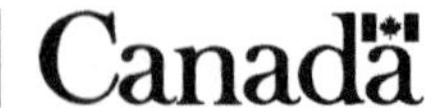
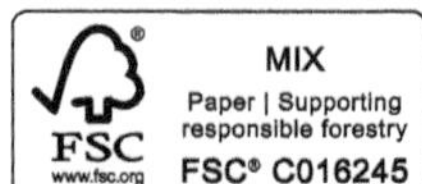

# Contents

vi | Contents

# Photographs and Exercises

## Photographs



## Exercises

# Acknowledgments

This book has been a labour of love, inspired by colleagues, friends, students, and mentors – I am grateful for your conversations, generosities, critiques, and provocations to think more expansively, create more experimentally, teach more generously, and act more thoughtfully at the intersections of art and life.

I want to give special thanks to the artists who allowed me to use their images in the book – and to the thinkers in the book who inspired me to push the limits of my own ideas about photography. Thanks to: Katherine Behar, Amanda Boetzkes, micha cárdenas, Mackenzie Gilstrap, Johnny Golding, Margret Grebowicz, Melissa Gueiros, Brandon Kan, Heather McAllister, Joyelle McSweeney, Simon Perez, and Andrea Wille.

A final thanks to the Simpson Center for the Humanities at the University of Washington for support of the project and to the University of Toronto Press – in particular, editors Stephen Jones and Mark Thompson – for believing in the manuscript and shepherding it through to publication. I am grateful for your support. Thanks always to Arthur Kroker, editor of the Digital Futures series in which this book appears.

A preliminary version of chapter 6 was published in *Baudrillard Now* 5, no. 1 (2024) as "Conspiracy Thinking: Towards an Ambiguous Theory of Photography."

Short sections drawn from the text have been compiled for publication as "Exercises for Seeing the Image Differently," in *The Analog Revisited: Questioning the Technical Image in a Digital Age*, edited by Renée C. Hoogland (Wilmington, DE: Vernon Press, forthcoming).

# PHOTOGRAPHING
# AMBIGUITY

# Introduction

## Provocation

What happens when all the photographs have been taken? When – as Jean Baudrillard prophesied – everything in the world, and maybe even things not in the world, has been captured by the camera?[1] Is this a prescient forecast of an algorithmic future in which the time between events and their pictures shrinks until it no longer makes sense to speak of a difference? A time when photographs are no longer necessary because life is already scripted entirely in advance. Predictive living.

Or is it something else? An absurdist misunderstanding, premised on the (perhaps mistaken) idea that the function of pictures is to dislocate the image from experience? For isn't the photograph a fantasy of memory – remembered the way a human never could – a once-lived moment preserved from the skewed vision of retrospect, the failing recall of biological minds, the distortions that happen when other people remember it differently? In short, a memory preserved from human tampering? This is the technical logic of photographic capture seen not for its data-driven ontology but instead charged with human mistrust of our own capacity to remember. The desire to preserve ourselves from ourselves is photographically (and technologically) significant. It is the human investment in the discourse of technicity – because of which we subject ourselves to externalized data standards in order to avoid confronting the ambiguities of subjective and partial understanding. To escape the human condition precisely by adopting non-human standards of evaluation – what Arthur Kroker eloquently termed the "will to technology" as the drive to quantify, evaluate, archive, and program[2] – all under the auspices of an informatic objectivity that finds **ambiguity**, **uncertainty**, and the **imagination** equally questionable because they fail to conform to the operational standards of appearance.

But just because technology doesn't admit to a positionality does not mean that it doesn't have one. That's the trouble with dominant ideologies after all – their pervasive presence makes them perversely invisible.

And so, a question: What would it mean to refuse this version of technology? To refuse the idea that quantification alone leads to valuable knowledge and to insist on preserving some of the more ambiguous spaces of lived reality – liminal ideas, strange positionalities, incommensurabilities and absurdities and failures and irrelevances and hacks and conspiracies and contaminations and falsities and imaginations and dreams? The result would have to be a form of photography that begins by disavowing the technical project of representation and instead focuses on the performance of that which can never be photographed – the ambiguities of lived encounter with individual worlds. To use the camera in this way would be to multiply the world – and in doing so prove that the world can be multiplied, that reality is neither unique nor self-evident, and that entanglements of bodies and images and imaginations are the ambiguous norm. *Photographing Ambiguity* proposes that images – despite appearances to the contrary – were never really meant to make sense of the world but rather to help make it stranger.

*Photographing Ambiguity* looks at photography as a metaphor for technological culture, arguing that a relational examination of the medium of photography can help us understand some of the dominant ideological tendencies of our times. In so doing, the book argues for uses of photography that can highlight and catalyse more ambiguous ways of relating to the world, suggesting that ambiguity is a way to cultivate more conscientious, ecological, relational, and creative relationships within the technological ecosystem of contemporary life. *Photographing Ambiguity* critiques the idea that images are best deployed to verify or document a world outside of us and proposes that such (quantifiable) ways of thinking – while rooted in the historical drive towards technology and data – have become so pervasive as to have become a dominant form of ideological bias in the twenty-first century. Against the ubiquity of data consciousness, this book proposes a series of exercises designed to cultivate an embodied encounter with digital living, not *against* the clouds of images, but *within* them – understanding photographs not as benchmarks of the real but as ambiguous constructions of the present and future imaginary.

## Lament

I used to lament the loss of the darkroom as the material counterpoint to the optical emphasis of the photographic medium. In my thinking, the darkroom was a site of blindness, characterized by exactly the opposite of sight – as a photographer develops film in the dark, waiting for the images to emerge, navigating by touch and memory rather than by optical markers of space. In short the darkroom was – to me – everything the camera wasn't (yet). A space of tactile mobility, not visual capture, where I had to feel my way around the room in the dark. Not a space of static visuality but of tactile mobility. A place of durations, not instants. A place of waiting, not capture. A place of imagination, not of finally resolved images.

Yes, navigating darkness used to be part of photography. Strange, right?

All this disappeared very suddenly with the advent of the digital image, and more so as the camera becomes increasingly ubiquitous and the image circulates at speeds that far surpass those of human vision. No more patience; in the competition between technical speed and human imagination, the question of duration has all but disappeared to the photographic equation. So too the question of the technical, subsumed into the ubiquity of portable devices of which the camera is simply one component. No more ambiguity either – the one-hour photo (which was already bad enough) replaced by the instant-gratification of mobile photography that entirely cuts out the process of waiting. And with it, the anticipation of the image – no more wondering or imagining if the pictures will turn out. Now we simply look and see (at best); often we don't even bother to verify. Post it and move on.

Yes, waiting used to be a part of photography. Strange, right?

But something happens when darkness disappears in this way – at least in my imagination of things. Squeezed out of the technical no less than the human, darkness finds its refuge in the very ideology of the system. In that classic postmodern way, darkness doesn't disappear because it is eradicated by the full-spectrum visuality of capture culture. Instead, darkness diffuses into the very fabric of a lived experience that will forever be in the dark – indeed that chooses the darkness as the only alternative to illuminated living. In a full capture system, darkness is the general state of human being, subjects as we are of the technical ideology of a system premised, on one hand, on the black-boxed technicality of increasingly automated and intelligent systems, and on the other, the imperative towards digital engagement where humans share publicly the things we like and fear, and in so doing also teach the algorithms how to better predict and service our daily lives.

We are not the ones watching anymore; we are learning sets for the intelligent systems of the future. Strange, right?

There is nothing ambiguous about the status of photography in a technological culture, except the actual status of lived human experience – either reducible to data points or economized by likes and shares, or perhaps something else. But what else is there? There is memory – perfectly imperfect as only a *human* system can be – and the camera as archive to preserve those moments we would otherwise fear losing. There is simulation, better than memory for its capacity to construct a staged and curated augmentation. There is novelty, a moment that might not ever have existed if someone hadn't suggested taking a picture, often moments of play or humour that wouldn't normally be considered real enough to make the curated archive of our lives. There is politics too – an attempt to establish a different set of evidence or documents or data points in the service of truth or rebellion or authenticity – to use the tools of capture against the system and document some of the other things still going on. So I guess there is something ambiguous about the status of photography after all, despite the fact that at first it doesn't seem so. Interesting right? That a medium so premised on clarity and disclosure might actually hide within it ambiguities of encounter and the possibility for thinking about the world a little bit differently.

It's not about what the camera does anymore. It's about the ways we build relationships with the ideologies that cameras set in motion.

## Structure

This book triangulates scholarly, artistic, and pedagogical concerns in a way that I believe offers an original, complex, and multifaceted contribution to the study of photography. As a scholar, I study digital culture, with a particular eye to the role of the imagination and creative thinking in the workings of technology. I am attentive to the impact of technology on the imagination – in ways that creatively expand the horizons of individual expression and paradoxically inhibit the mind from imagining in other ways. As an artist I engage these questions in practice, thinking about images for their performative and inductive capacities. Pictures have the capacity to imagine possible escape routes from the realities of the everyday, or to reconfigure relationships to individual and collective communities – but they also have the ability to create and sustain fantasies and falsities in ways that are both dangerous and powerful. As a teacher I guide others towards these nuances and complexities, rarely making attempts to resolve the paradoxes and ambiguities of the camera – quite the opposite. Given recent quests for non-human and post-human ways of thinking about technology, I think a required first step (following Karen Barad,[3] Donna Haraway,[4] Joanna Zylinska,[5] and others) is to renounce the self-evidence of the image and to instead recognize the entanglements, paradoxes, conspiracies, and manipulations that pictures are capable of producing. The challenge that this presents, from my perspective, is that of imagining beyond horizons of coherent thought, since what is at stake is precisely the camera's capacity to create affective and performative relationships that are not accountable to coherence (which is not to say that they are incoherent, necessarily, though they might be). My focus embraces the irreducibility of experience, siding with practice, performance, and relationality as ways of engaging with photographs without trying to construct a new ontology of the image.

To this end, *Photographing Ambiguity* takes a catalytic form, pairing photographic exercises (developed as pedagogical tools and expanded into a public digital archive) with a discussion of important contemporary thinkers at the intersection of questions of technology, ecology, and politics. The exercises insist on a performative understanding of photography – that is, that by implicating oneself in certain forms of technical performance, it is possible to discover new insights into what it means to live with pictures. The thinkers provide conceptual counterpoints to the exercises, each in essence providing a new context in which to consider the formal workings and social consequences of photography. The result is not intended to be a new theory of photography but rather a supplemental series of speculations, provocations, and possible other ways to conceptualize the role and relevance of the contemporary image.

To elaborate, the exercises in the book are conceptualized as "response projects," and they are designed to help see the world differently by asking us to represent it differently. These projects aim to dislodge regular ways of looking, and in so doing they call on us to reexamine the extent to which we rely on habit and convention in our everyday interactions. By proposing these exercises I invite a form of practice-based inquiry, hoping to catalyse a conversation about what photographs do – and how we, as makers of images (artists and otherwise) might understand some of the subtle and implicit nuances of the medium such as to expand our possibilities for creative engagement with pictures. While many of the "learning objectives" of these exercises are self-evident, from my perspective the invitation to explore photography through acts of actually taking pictures constitutes a perspective quite different from traditional theorizations of the image, which largely focus on analysis and often (from my perspective) ignore the importance of incorporating new structures of thought into the actual practice of making and circulating pictures. The idea of practice-based learning is not new; what is new, however, is the insistence that photography today is best understood from its ubiquitous inside, challenging not just how we think about images but how the pictures we take tend to uphold certain documentary or representational conventions. That is, the practice of picture taking seems, to me, misaligned with many of the ways in which pictures are thought. This book asks us to hold practice and theory together, leveraging the differences between engagement and ideology in order to propose alternate ways to think about and make photographs.

Likewise, the thinkers I have chosen to focus on are not those that one might expect for a book of this sort. While I invoke many canonized and established voices of photographic thinking (specifically Paul Virilio, Peter Sloterdijk, Roland Barthes, François Laruelle, Vliém Flusser, and Jean

Baudrillard), the main focus of the text is not on disputing past ways of conceptualizing the image. Rather, I am interested in speculative possibilities for understanding photography differently – the ways in which the image can be seen as a complex marker of technical ideology and a prophet of the technological future, and how the increasing ubiquity and performativity of the picture infiltrates other kinds of conversations. Images are not just part of our visual world; they are part of our minds, part of how we self-conceive, part of how we relate to others, part of how we imagine – and equally part of how we politic and play. The thinkers I have chosen highlight this technological ecosystem in their work, situating their own concerns at intersections with image culture: **Amanda Boetzkes**, an art historian who specializes in questions of technology and ecology; **Joyelle McSweeney**, a poet and inventor of the "necro-pastoral"; **Margret Grebowicz**, best known for her work on national parks and whales; **micha cárdenas**, a digital media artist working at the fringes of blurred virtual and material boundaries; **Katherine Behar**, artist and founder of object-oriented feminism; and **Johnny Golding**, a feminist philosopher of technology and radical materiality.

Pairing these thinkers with my photographic exercises, the hope is to bring complexity into the conversation while featuring other distinct ways of conceptualizing the image – each revealing a strategy for making pictures more ambiguous, and in the process more alive, more relational, more reflective, ecological, creative, responsive, and dialogic.

## Snapshots

*Photographing Ambiguity* is organized into six self-con-tained chapters that unfold as a series of conceptual por-traits of the image. The idea of series is important to me: Working in series is one of the first (photographic) meth-ods I teach my students, and I want to explore it in this book as an operative metaphor for the text as well. In a series, photographers repeat their methods but with dif-ferent subjects, holding space for different iterations of similar ideas. In an analogous way, the chapters in this book are not organized according to an argumentative arc, nor designed to particularly build on each other – they are similar but different articulations of the larger concept of photographing ambiguity. There is thus a certain seriality – even a formulaic quality – to the way the book is imagined. Each chapter opens with an artistic exercise designed to catalyse different (performative) ways of conceptualizing the image. An example from the project is shown, and I provide a short written reflection that I see as a model for critical engagement with images in our current moment.[6] Main themes from the exercise are then used to juxtapose a canonical thinker of photography (most of them post-modern and post-structural thinkers) with more contem-porary, queer, feminist, situated, and politically engaged thinkers of culture and technology. The aim is to update, complicate, elaborate, and disorient some of the standard-ized ways of thinking the picture by inflecting the discus-sion with thoughts drawn from cutting-edge thinkers of the technological, ecological, and artistic trajectories of our times. The chapters end with a return to the exercise used to catalyse the discussion, holding together the artistic and the theoretical in order to reiterate the larger commitment of this text to a kind of ambiguity that can encourage readers to locate themselves and their own relationships to visual and digital culture.

In the following pages, I offer a series of snapshots of chapters as a way to introduce the method and mood of the text. In a sense, this is a "contact sheet" for the book, an abridged summary from which additional details will be expanded and enlarged.[7]

Chapter 1, "Ecopoetics of Blur," begins with the invitation to photograph someone with their eyes crossed, an action that the political theorist and arts activist Serena Kataoka credits with opening up new ways of seeing the world.[8] Foregrounding the relationship between a focussed camera lens and a purposefully unfocused human gaze also makes clear that there is an explicit power dynamic at play between the two: the human gaze held accountable to technological standards of vision and not the other way around. This chapter links the technicity of vision to the question of ecopoetics and ecological thinking, focusing on the work of Amanda Boetzkes, especially her books *The Ethics of Earth Art* and *Plastic Capitalism*.[9] In these works Boetzkes argues for what she calls the "ecologicity" of thought – that is, an attentiveness to the relationships between technology and ecology.[10] My interest is specifically in applying Boetzkes's theory of ecological thinking to the question of photography, here arguing that a technologically imposed standard of focused vision betrays other forms of human and non-human perception in ways that foreclose on different understandings of the relationship between individuals, images, and larger social and ecological contexts. To make this observation is to politicize the camera – not only for the principle of objectification that governs photographic capture, but more fundamentally for the technicity of vision that it imposes on human ideology. Cameras pre-focus the human gaze, an observation well-stated by Paul Virilio,[11] but given a more contemporary urgency by Boetzkes. To look at the world with crossed eyes is a metaphor for ecological complexity – it could be called an **ecopoetics of blur**. *Against the hegemony of focused observation, a meditation on the power and possibilities of blurred vision.*

Chapter 2, "Necro-Reflectivity," begins with the proposition to take a mirror for a walk, inviting contemplation of the French writer and literary critic Stendhal's (Marie-Henri Beyle) assertion that "the novel is a mirror one walks along a path."[12] Repositioning a literal connection between the image and reflection, the project offers a forum in which to think about the circulation of images and the economy of reflection and reflectivity, noting that one irony of visual culture is that – without the mediating apparatuses of camera and mirror – the only thing that has no visual presence to us is ourselves. Focusing on Joyelle McSweeney's discussion of the "necropastoral" as a contemporary mode of artistic and political engagement,[13] the chapter builds a theory of necro-reflectivity as a strategy for understanding the refracted identities of image culture. For McSweeney, the necropastoral is "necro" because it problematizes the boundaries between the living and the undead, acknowledging the environmental, social, and political crises that govern our times while insisting on the urgency of locating creative individual presences. There is a performative edge to this idea, one that shares much with Peter Sloterdijk's critique of objective distance and his proposal for a "critical proximity" between thought and action.[14] McSweeney goes further, however, to fuse proximity and politics, bound together in an aesthetics of dissent that no longer privileges the discourses of (human-centred) life over those of the non-living (or differently-alive).[15] Between McSweeney and Sloterdijk, then, a theory of **necro-reflectivity** emerges as a strategically performative use of the camera to re-cast reflective relationships to the world. *Against the ideology of critical distance, a conscientious attempt to implicate oneself in the relational presence of images.*

Chapter 3, "Smash Metaphysics," opens with an exercise in which participants are asked to break something and then take its picture. The point is to emphasize the implicit relationship between the violence of the image and the technological performance of picture taking. That is, the point of the project is to insist on the photographic act as metaphysically distinct from simply the act of looking, requiring a particular way of engaging the world (as an object to be photographed) and oneself (as an agent of objectification). Focusing on the work of Margret Grebowicz, and in particular her books *The National Park to Come* and *Whale Song*, this chapter explores a theatrical tendency of the camera and its relationship to the socialization of technological culture. For Grebowicz, national parks are sites whose complex identities are upheld by acts of politics, faith, and photography –

situated in the liminal spaces between nostalgia and simulation that form what she calls a "geography of hope."[16] And the role of the photograph in this matrix is to not to document the authenticity of nature but to permit us to forget the impact of technological and human mediation on the natural world. There is a relationship here to Roland Barthes's provocative insistence that photography is not a representational medium, but one whose ambitions are more in line with the theatrical.[17] In ways that extend Barthes's argument, Grebowicz notes a futuristic ontology of the image, one that is decidedly not about a nostalgia for the past but about an affective simulation of futurity.[18] Between Grebowicz and Barthes, then, emerges a proposal for what might be called **smash metaphysics** as a performance of photography designed to disclose the theatricality of the image. *Against the assumption of images as representational, a staging of affect as effect and an embracing of photography as a theatrical art.*

Chapter 4, "Non-Choreography," opens with an exercise in which participants are asked to take a photograph of somebody wearing a chair on their head. The project is an homage to the novel *Au Plafond* (*On the Ceiling*) by the French author Éric Chevillard, who mobilizes the chair as a prosthetic to correct bad physical posture.[19] In the exercise, the chair becomes a metaphor for bad imaginative posture – and a challenge to think beyond the assumed (correct) uses of everyday objects which implicitly choreograph our behavioural and performative relationships. The argument is expanded with reference to the writing of micha cárdenas, and in particular the concept of the "transreal," which she uses to explore the shifting boundaries of the real and the virtual and – importantly – the link of these categories to that of performance.[20] Performance is, for cárdenas, a guarantee of embodied presence that can be so important to the question of digital culture because it insists on locating the individual within the technological matrix. This is proximity taken to the next level, immersive engagement that cannot really be thought of as detached from reality because immersion is how realities – virtual or otherwise – are created, what cárdenas calls "explicit reality construction."[21] To think of the performative and the virtual in this way is to echo François Laruelle's call for a "non-philosophical" way of thinking, in which philosophy loses sight of itself through performative proximity.[22] The result is philosophical action, or what Laruelle calls non-philosophy (or non-photography, when it applies to the image).[23] Between cárdenas and Laruelle, then, emerges a proposal for a sort of **non-choreography** that can challenge the behaviour scripts that tend to mark technological engagement by insisting on a creative proximity to the performance of digital interaction. *Against the scripting of technological behaviours, an absurdist choreography of engagement.*

Chapter 5, "Digital Darkness," opens with the provocation to point a laser pointer at a camera, an act that creates a lens flare that over-exposes the technological sensor, effectively blinding the camera in the process. Inspired by the philosopher Vilém Flusser's assertion that technology has a tendency to over-write human ways of understanding the world,[24] this project looks for ways to speak back to the systems that code our ways of knowing and behaving. In a sense, this simple act is one that makes a camera self-aware, forced to confront a certain limitation of its own optical capacity to focus. The exercise is expanded through a discussion of the work of Katherine Behar, particularly focused on her analysis of big data and "object-oriented feminism"[25] through which Behar develops her concept of "decelerationist aesthetics."[26] Like Flusser, Behar is attentive to the limits and pressures of technological systems, pushing for forms of ambiguity and vagueness that defy operationalization to the extent that they allow for a re-imagining (and a slowing down) of the ways in which technology creates and represents the worlds we inhabit. In a digital age, the kind of darkness that historically existed in absence of light no longer really exists. Instead, in a technological culture darkness needs to be manufactured, created, engendered, or performed – largely through the embracing of excess and over-exposure as new forms of **digital darkness**. *Against the objectivity of illuminated appearances, a theory of overexposure.*

Chapter 6, "Conspiracy Thinking," opens with an invitation to wear a tinfoil hat for the camera, a project inspired by Julian Huxley's 1927 story "The Tissue King," about a machine designed as an experimental mind control apparatus.[27] To protect themselves from the telepathic broadcast, the inventors of the machine wore aluminium hats, specifically designed to protect their minds from the penetrating forces of cognitive manipulation. Against the backdrop of Huxley's story, this chapter explores the speculative and conjectural possibilities of conspiracy theory, gravitating towards a performative understanding of data (and images) for the behaviours it provokes rather than the truth or falsity of its claims. More important than truth or falsity is how data is made to matter – an idea expounded through the doubled lens of Jean Baudrillard's provocative claims about the conspiracy of the real[28] and Johnny Golding's eloquent meditations on the "radical mattering" of experiential and collaborative action.[29] The fate of photography seen in this way is to occupy the position of conspiracy theorist – not in a cynical sense but rather as a conspiring agent working with others to create alternate contexts for engagement (and representation). Collaboration – perhaps even friendship – is the bottom line, and thus also the new rule of image culture – avoiding the question of truth and reality allows for a licence to collectively reimagine the terms of engagement for life itself. *Against the profiling of digitally-composed subjectivity, a theory that conspires towards a form of performative collectivity.*

The book concludes with the challenge to photograph the imagination directly, without the intermediary space of materiality – to take a photograph directly from the mind. The project recreates an experiment in psychic photography conducted by Ted Serios in the 1960s, in which Serios claimed to be able to project his mind directly onto film.[30] In a digital era, filled with brainwave visualization software and enhanced biometric capture systems, the challenge is perhaps less absurd than it was for Serios, but a bottom line question remains: if one hasn't tried it for oneself, how does one know it's not possible? And that's really the bottom line for this book as well. Joseph Beuys once proclaimed that everyone is an artist and that we are collectively creating our future social order.[31] I think he's right, but my aspiration here is more humble. Everyone is a photographer – indeed cameras have become ubiquitous to the point where it's no longer self-evident if or how pictures and life can be separated in any real or meaningful way. It's also no longer clear what one teaches when one teaches photography – especially if one is teaching to the current moment rather than to the now historical practices of darkroom processes and chemical printing. Photography today is instant, user-friendly, and ubiquitous – and the challenge of understanding the image isn't at all one of knowing how to make it better or more effective. Nobody cares. It's about what it means to live within an image matrix, an environment – indeed an ecology – of pictures circulating at the speed of influence, which is to say at the speed of attention and mood and popularity and dreams and possibilities and whatever other stories we tell ourselves about the visual landscapes in which life unfolds. And so – influence is key. For Serios it was influencing the camera. For me that story might be more metaphoric than aspirational, but it nonetheless does a good job of representing the stakes of the contemporary image, in all its wonderful possibilities for ambiguity.

## Photographing Ambiguity

An initial reviewer of this book suggested that the text would benefit from a more concise and specific definition of what it was I meant by ambiguity. I prefer to let ambiguity remain ambiguous. I feel quite strongly about it, in fact. For, in an age of definitions, technical solutions, operational logics, efficiency algorithms, and productivity metrics, if it's no longer possible to hold space for concepts that don't have clear or delineated boundaries, I think we have a problem. But I actually don't think we have a problem – I think ambiguities are all around us, they just don't get the recognition they deserve. But the point here – and the politic if I were to really plant my stance – is that there would be no worse insult to the concept of ambiguity than to concisely and specifically define it. It would be the total betrayal of the concept itself.

For me, this is not just a rhetorical insistence. I see ambiguity as representative of a category of concepts that share this incongruency between definition and manifestation, a category of concepts that I believe might benefit from a more nuanced form of engagement. I think of the concept of creativity as a parallel (but slightly different) example. For creativity the problem is not the precision of a definition but the fact that definitions themselves are decidedly uncreative by nature, designed as they are to standardize meaning rather than open it up. To subject creativity to a standardized definition in which there are no creative variations seems to me quite awful, and definitely counter to the spirit of creativity itself. I might say the same of the concept of uncertainty, which – when defined – loses the uncertain quality it is meant to represent. For me, there is an important acknowledgment to be made here – allowing concepts to retain a form of identity that is congruous with the philosophical spaces they are meant to hold. To allow the status of uncertainty to be itself uncertain; to allow creativity to apply itself to its own definition; to honour the spirit of ambiguity for the ways it can hold meaningful space without needing to argue or clearly articulate its agenda. Against the tendency to document, quantify, objectify, an attempt to engage concepts on their own provocative terms.

This is not to say that concepts like ambiguity and creativity should be left unaccountable – nothing further from the sort. I simply think a different form of accountability is needed for these kinds of concepts, one – I would propose – not grounded in technical definitions of informatic standardization but rather in community. Creativity appears differently in different communities – and I think that's great. The same for ambiguity, and often the spaces of ambiguity cultivate conversations that would not have happened otherwise.

And so – photographing ambiguity as a way to build communities that can begin to imagine the image differently. Less an external standard or a horizon of accountability. More a conversation about how to creatively re-make the world in ways that appreciate the ambiguities of existence, especially those least disposed to a technical rendering. It's ambiguous on purpose.

# 1

# Ecopoetics of Blur

**Exercise 1: Take a Picture of Someone with Their Eyes Crossed**

**Framing statement:** In his novel *A Journey to Ixtlan*, Carlos Castaneda describes a conversation with an Indigenous sorcerer who teaches him to see the world differently. The technique "consisted of gradually forcing your eyes to see separately the same image. The lack of image conversion entailed a double perception of the world ... which the eyes were ordinarily incapable of perceiving."[1] Seeing the world with crossed eyes, for Castaneda, was a first step towards a larger understanding of vision, multiplied out of the linearity of bifocal sight.

In her essay "Feeling with Your Eyes," artist and activist Serena Kataoka takes this notion one step further, arguing that Castaneda's notion of cross-eyed vision can also be applied to social and political culture, allowing one to hold multiple – and sometimes conflicting – perspectives in one's mind at the same time.[2] In Kataoka's view, one might see in two different ways out of two different eyes – not simply a difference in optics but potentially one with ideological implications, quite literally allowing for new ways of thinking to emerge. Or proposing the possibility of seeing multiple versions of the world, held together by blur instead of by the usual tropes of focused singular vision.

**Guidelines:** With Castaneda and Kataoka in mind, this project holds visual space for the idea of seeing the world differently, exploring what it would mean for a subject to choose the blurriness of vision instead of optical focus. To participate, take a portrait-style photograph of someone with their eyes crossed. The image stands as a metaphor for seeing in more than one way at a time – and for seeing in ways that cameras cannot accomplish on their own – contributing to a growing archive that will poetically stand for multiple ways of perceiving the world.

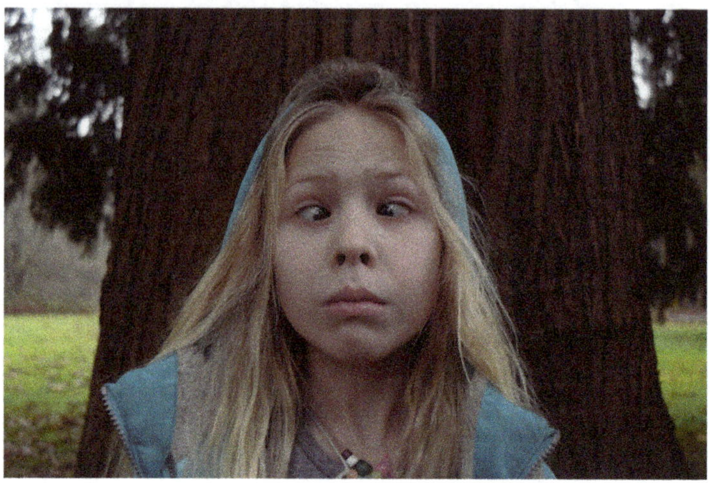

Figure 1. Mackenzie Gilstrap, *Cross-Eyed Visions*, photograph, 2017

## Cross-Eyed Visions

A young girl stands, hooded, facing the camera, with her eyes crossed. Behind her looms a large tree. It feels like a second hood that is more than simply a backdrop to the portrait. This tree is almost a shadow, almost a building, almost a guardian, almost a menace. It is something, but I feel it more than I see it – at least at first. The tree sets the mood, even though it is not really it that I see. I see a girl with her eyes crossed.

Usually when looking at pictures the eye will focus on what is already in focus. But here I find my eyes confused, focusing on what is in focus (optically) but not itself focused in a regular way. What I see is what I do not see: I see someone not looking at me. A portrait of a person facing the camera but not looking at the lens, or rather looking twice such that the lens might reside in between other things she sees. I see that I do not see what she sees.

Perhaps she's playing a game, wondering if – when she crosses her eyes – the camera can still see her? My look follows her gaze to … somewhere not really in the picture: a space between herself and the camera, the tip of her nose or just beyond. If she is aware of the camera at all it would be out of the peripheral vision of each of her eyes, two cameras – one on each side of wherever she is actually looking. It shuts down something about how I am used to cameras working. I am used to a camera showing a world that sees me the same way I see it. So what is this gesture, this crossing of eyes, this insistence on a certain kind of invisibility that is also a refusal to be as one is seen?

But that's interesting. Can crossing one's eyes at the camera be seen as a resistance tactic? If so, then in order to really understand this picture, it is necessary to abandon the stability of what is represented and to instead adopt its posture. That is, while it may be a strange proposition to make, this picture may be best appreciated by crossing one's own eyes. The resulting image will not render in the normal way, will not reconcile two parallax visions into one – and perhaps that's the point. Parallax is an evolutionary function designed for the perception of depth. But a photograph has no depth; and one does not need depth perception to look at a picture. The background sits on the same flat surface as the young girl's nose. To insist that one needs depth perception in order to see a photograph is to misunderstand the opportunity an image presents – the possibility of seeing two worlds instead of just one.

There is no depth, but as a result I feel free to see things other than the image itself – to see, perhaps, its idea. I cross my eyes and I see two young girls, facing me (the camera) with crossed eyes. Behind them looms a tree. In front of them looms … well, me.

## Between Crossed Eyes

Sometimes moments invite being seen with crossed eyes – marked by a kind of dissatisfaction with regular appearances and a need to make vision excessive – twice the world means no singular identities, no fixed or static objects, thus the possibility for different ways of seeing. It makes no sense to just try to re-focus; focus was the problem. Better to explore modes of engaging without focus – aim in between the multiple pictures of the world and simply take a step. I don't recommend doing it while driving, but when walking down the street the worst that will happen is a soft collision with a lamp post or another human. It is actually surprising how much of the world still makes sense when walking in this way. Without "things" to guide one's movement, the world becomes a site of negotiation and navigation, an immersive environment that shifts and demands constant attention. This does not seem like a bad thing to me. It puts the human on the responsive. Sometimes two versions are better than one.

When I was a graduate student, Donna Haraway gave a lecture at the Pacific Centre for Technology and Culture, eloquently sharing ideas from her *Companion Species Manifesto*.[3] I've always loved what I see as Haraway's insistence on locating relationships within a matrix of power, extending this to the argument that for dogs (in her case – but of course much more generally applicable) are not humans, cannot be treated as humans, and new terms of interspecies engagement need to be negotiated for any possibility of true companionship.[4] It was an argument that resonated – though one question from a student sticks with me. The student – I think hoping for affirmation – asked about hugging trees as a way to connect to the non-human world. Haraway scoffed, caught herself, and then told the student that a core sample would give her better information about the tree.

The student was disappointed. I was too, but not because I thought it wrong – just uncreative. Haraway preferred the quantifiability of scientific harvest to the ethical questionability of anthropomorphism. But the more of her work I read, the more I wonder if Haraway *now* would still agree with Haraway *then*, particularly given her recent work on "staying with the trouble" as a way to avoid reproducing dominant logics of knowledge production?[5] Haraway then called herself a natural scientist; Haraway now writes collaborative science fiction. These of course are not mutually exclusive activities, but I need to expand (or double) my imagination of her work in order to hold both in my attention at the same time. I find it hard to believe that collaborative science fiction would discount the merit of hugging trees (though it might critique the anthropocentric expectation that a tree would – or could – hug back). I ask myself if there is "trouble" in hugs, and if so, is it the kind to "stay with" or to dismiss as not serious enough to form a relational basis for engagement?

Consider the possibility that trees actually do hug – they just take a really long time to do it, growing branches and roots that embrace the world around them in ways that are hard to deny. If I wanted a hug from a tree, could I hold still – could I hold my (human) self accountable – "staying with" the time it takes for a tree to embrace in this way? The ivy in my backyard grows pretty fast; maybe that's a good place to begin. It's a blurring of the boundaries within the hierarchy of anthropomorphic thought, putting the human on the responsive. I would call it an ecopoetics of blur – a lived stance achieved by blurring relational boundaries of the encountered world.

Ecopoetics of blur? Isn't that what happens when one decentres a human vision of the world in order to try and reconceptualize what it means to live relationally on a troubled planet? **Cross-eyed visions** is not just a game of doubled vision but a procedural metaphor for de-centring human linearity in order to insert oneself in a world seen always in (at least) two ways at the same time.

## The Accident of Humanity

I find it interesting that a photograph can lead to an argument for hugging trees – an unlikely phenomenological proposition grown from a technical reflection about the limits of technicity. A focused image that cultivates sensitivity to blur. I might call it a form of what the philosopher and art historian Amanda Boetzkes calls "ecologicity," the act of "attuning vision to an ecological reality."[6] Only this time ecology and technology are conflated in ways reminiscent of Paul Virilio's pronouncements on the accident implicit in all technological systems – but in reverse. If for Virilio all technology carries within it an accident waiting to happen (the loss of blurred awareness being perhaps the accident of focused vision, for instance),[7] for Boetzkes something a bit more complicated happens – the accident is what requires new forms of environmental self-reflexivity.[8]

## The Provocation

What would happen if we thought of Amanda Boetzkes as the ecological update to Paul Virilio, focusing not on accidents to come but on one that has already happened? That is, where for Virilio the accident is the latent destiny of every technology, for Boetzkes the accident is the ecology of the present technological moment. When one invents humanity, one invents the end of the natural world. And what would then happen if we tried to extradite this in photographic ways – to think photography as an environmental practice to the extent that it has a reflective relationship to that which is represented. Every photograph an accident. The Anthropocene as the accident of humanity itself.

## The Short Form

**Amanda Boetzkes** is a Canadian art historian and the star of this juxtaposition, a rare intellectual mind that pushes the boundaries between art, technology, and philosophy while insisting on a new metaphysics of ecological conscience. Boetzkes inspires me with the ways she attunes to the structures of power created by ideology – how one thinks predicates possible ways of perceiving and interacting with the world. For Boetzkes, to truly understand the question of technology (or art), it is essential to understand it with an ecological conscience. But that's just the starting point, since ecology happens always in an already compromised context, where it's not just about best practices but about grief and the acknowledgment of complicity in a world one has helped to create. For Boetzkes, how one represents this situation matters, for the plasticity of representation (and the representation of plasticity) holds the key to rethinking the role of the human on a trajectory towards extinction.

**Paul Virilio** is a French philosopher who charms and alarms me with his theories of technological prosthesis: his deep lament for the ways that technological facility comes at the expense of human capacity. In a way, Virilio is a thinker of limits – insightful for the ways he understands technology as always transgression of the human, and always returning to the body itself as the most material of existential sites. For me, Virilio is the last humanist – and his work thus a thorough taxonomy of ways in which the human spirit and imagination has been seduced, co-opted, transgressed, and hijacked by twenty-first-century technological culture. Manifest, I think, most powerfully in his condemnation of contemporary art,[9] Virilio does not pull back when it comes to conflating technological insight and ethical judgment, instead insisting on a certain morality to even the most aestheticized of practices – ones that often disappoint him in ways that I find haunting.

What I'm proposing, then, is to consider Boetzkes as the twenty-first-century answer to Virilio – a thinker who shares his spirit of critique but with a new pragmatics that eschews the lament for a lost humanity in favour of thinking what it means to live, at the same time, ecologically and post-humanly (if not properly posthumously). That is – what haunts Virilio's thought is the possibility of a future that is already Boetzkes's present moment, and probably ours as well – filled with social, political, and ecological ghosts that we cannot simply walk away from (that's what makes them haunting, after all) and so must find ways to live with and within. The accident has already happened, and it is not the shock of the accident that motivates insight but a reconciliation to the pragmatic truth of living after the disaster itself. When one walks among ghosts, much of what appears does so with a certain blur.

## Stealing Souls

There is a story – not really an urban myth; probably more a colonial romanticism – that cameras steal souls. And I am superstitious (or at least I am trying to be), so I actually think it's true. The tricky thing – as near as I can tell – is that it works counter-intuitively. Consider, for instance, the way a vaccination injects a small amount of a virus into a body and thus creates the conditions for virus recognition and an ability to manufacture antibodies. I see pictures that way – creating a context for social and technological recognition beyond the constraints of embodied living. Certainly images desensitize bodies to the ever-increasing ubiquity of visual impact – each exposure a booster in the process of inoculating individuals, numbing the effects of image culture as a whole. But strangely it also works the other way around, decentring the individual in ways that are only possible because individuality (and perhaps even the soul) was never bound to the body to begin with – at least not in a visual form; always a phantom double. The camera is a truly occult device, stealing souls not by removing them from a body but by multiplying them – so many distributed pieces of each individual soul that the idea of a singular or self-contained spirit becomes instantly tangled in the dynamics of proliferating multiplicity. Images change the very make-up of the bodies with which they interact.

The thinker that frames this relationship most forcibly for me has always been Paul Virilio, for whom the case is much more dire; the photograph standing as exemplary technology and metaphor for the technological domination of the human spirit itself. In no uncertain terms, Virilio believes that technology colonizes the human body and mind – with documentary truth and precision information as its weapons, stealing souls (along with our sight and our minds) in the process.[10] This because, for Virilio, any time a technology begins to exceed human capacity (which he theorizes as the dominant trend of the twentieth century) it replaces humanly observable standards with new computational criteria thought more efficiently, more precisely, more objectively and thus less subject to human spirit or nuance.[11] The standards according to which humanity thus becomes subject are literally not observable to humans themselves without the enhanced capacity of technological systems. "The watching gaze has long since ceased to be that of the artist or even the scientist, but belongs to the instruments of technological vision."[12] I share his feeling that photography provides an anticipatory logic for the rise of computational thinking.

Nowhere is this more pronounced for Virilio than in contemporary art, where photographs often break from their documentary impulse in the attempt to create new (technical and technological) futures. When representation becomes "presentative" no more are we – for Virilio – living in times of knowledge and science, but in an age of soullessness (to be fair he calls is pitilessness) characterized by abuses of power and an absence of empathy towards others.[13] The most powerful example of this, for me, has always been Virilio's meditation on the disappearance of silence in the late twentieth century, what he calls the "silencing of silence."[14] In a fast-paced world of technological acceleration, noise abounds – often the digital hum of electronic technology. Silence is hard to find but easy to manufacture in the form of white noise machines, noise-cancelling headphones, and ear plugs – all designed not to reintroduce environmental silence but to forcibly (and for Virilio, violently) cancel out noise. That is, no more passive silence as a result of stillness or reflective thought; silence now is an active force of cancellation – a technologically produced architecture in the form of wearable devices and elevator music, all designed to actively silence the sounds of the world.

And the same for the soul – well, my soul at least – which now circulates online and on phones and in albums and printed on walls. Bits of my soul everywhere, sometimes anticipating my arrival, sometimes content to have me not-present – present-enough by virtue of a picture. This economy of souls is not just a dynamic of power (though it is that too). It is, more importantly perhaps, a context. This is lived reality – I don't and can't see myself everywhere I am present. I don't and can't see from all my eyes. Those eyes of mine that circulate in the world are literally sightless – and even my own embodied eyes, when compared to the systems that register truth for the world, belong to that category of vision that Virilio calls "sightless":

> Blindness is thus very much at the heart of the coming "vision machine." The production of *sightless vision* is itself merely the reproduction of an intense blindness that will become the latest and last form of industrialization: the *industrialization of the non-gaze*.[15]

If this image isn't haunting, it should be – souls that have left their bodies to roam, and to fraternize with anti-bodies. Imagine if souls preferred anti-bodies to bodies, recapturing a vaccine imagination in which the world inoculates itself from me by virtue of my image. It would be an accident of the vaccine, of course – not what a photograph was designed to do.[16] But if the photograph was intended to authenticate and validate, it was only ever because those sentiments bore precarity in times past. No more; now it is the body that is precarious in the face of its image. Virilio recounts: "at the end of the Gulf War, forty Iraqi soldiers surrendered to a drone. Surrendering to a flying camera is a terrifying image."[17] Anyone who thinks cameras can't steal souls has never imagined a photograph as surrender.

## Peripheral Visioning

Birds aren't real. They are another elaborate hoax designed to dupe us into thinking nature is natural and the planet isn't really dying. As the story goes, birds are actually surveillance drones, cleverly disguised as animals such as to make sure that nothing ever goes unseen. This, at least, according to the "Birds Aren't Real" website, which markets conspiracy and irony in equal measure.[18] But it's a perfect proposition for the times in which we live where it's difficult not to acknowledge the full double bind that cameras create. For one, surely surrender to a camera must now be seen not only as a wartime nightmare but as an everyday occurrence. Pictures permit entry into official culture: from driver's licences to passports, from social media accounts to online networked connectivity, from surveillance cameras to storefront CCTV. No more does my image simply document me – it is what allows passage into the networks of technological living. Being photographed is not optional, it is mandatory and celebrated and called participatory citizenship. I surrender to the culture of images, and as a consequence, being photographed ceases to be an event. It is instead the expected context for a general state of living.

And thus Birds Aren't Real as a simulacrum that stands extreme to help also position a cynical alternative, a form of ecological attention to image culture that can only really be understood by broadening the critical context in environmental ways. What is needed is a technocultural form of what Amanda Boetzkes calls "ecologicity" – a concept grown from her analysis of contemporary earth art as a form of engagement with the potential to develop new forms of environmental conscience.[19] For Boetzkes, earth art – at its best – holds the capacity to engage with natural environments without violating them, a form of what Lucy Irigaray calls "recessive ethics," here deployed towards displacing the colonial obsession with the domination of nature in favour of an engagement (in earth art) of what it means to be situated in relation to that which one does not or cannot know.[20] Recessive ethics requires this acknowledgment as a foundational tenet of respect for those with which one engages; for Boetzkes, to make or think about earth art is to require an ecological posture.[21]

In this, I follow Boetzkes's refusal of what she calls the "false dichotomy" between "the particular concerns of the environmental and the complex identities that stem from global interconnectivity."[22] And I transpose her arguments about environmental conscience (at the end of the world) to my own understanding of living in a world that has fully surrendered to the image. As Boetzkes puts it, "In the study of earth art lie the terminologies for how we might re-imagine our relationship to the planet."[23] And in the study of pictures lie the terminologies for re-imagining our relationship to image culture – no longer simply seeing what is presented in front of us, but that which is on the periphery too, even if it cannot be seen with the same clarity of focus, even if it sees us more than we see it.

I see this as a decidedly new form of environmental consciousness, one that is sensitive to the pervasiveness of the image, what Boetzkes pointedly calls "an ecological understanding of technology."[24] Virilio would call this an "inverted miracle" (for him, among the worst possible outcomes of technological trajectory) – an accident that has risen to contextual, even ecological proportions.[25] But if I am to take seriously the attempt to merge Boetzkes's theorization of earth art and my examination of the photograph, it becomes necessary to be unambiguous about the ambiguity this creates for the question of the image. The clarity of an image belies the ambiguity of context, which is sometimes blurry and complex and other times entirely fabricated. But one thing is certain: if the Anthropocene is a human fabrication of geological scale, then it's certainly not controversial to suggest that image culture is an actual environment in ways that require ecological (not technological) thought. Images are already always part of the technological ecosystem within which contemporary urban life unfolds.

To see it in this way requires a certain conceptual abstraction that blurs the difference between the contextual and the ecological. It is a visual climate instilled by the slippery rise of image culture into the place where it comes to dominate forms of human imagination. I would call it peripheral visioning, noting out of the corners of our eyes the birds that fly by and realizing that – real or not – they are part of our same surveillance ecology of contemporary urban living. I surrender to the birds that aren't real.

## Plastic Gaia

Images aren't images. They are ideological constructs that circulate as representations of themselves. Eco-chambers, circulating through a system of bodies and minds. Images are energy; they are currency, but they are also currents in an electrical sense: they have a charge. Or an odour. They have something – probably metaphoric – that isn't what they claim to have but that is at least as potent. Or maybe it's less potent and more pollutant, following Boetzkes's idea of pollution "as a way to appropriate the planet, in much the same way that animals mark their territory through bodily excretions."[26] Now that's a nice idea: images as bodily excretions. It's the opposite of surrender; it's a scrappy form of re-territorialization – marking out a sort of virtual contour of photographed encounter. The problem is that the image doesn't care; images assume surrender – that's the way dominant logics work. More a museum than a territory. That which fails to submit becomes garbage.

But maybe these are not incompatible observations, insofar as Boetzkes – in her book *Plastic Capitalism: Contemporary Art and the Drive to Waste* – offers a theorization of garbage that articulates a certain form of counterintuitive agency. Garbage assumes consumption; in fact, waste is the performative guarantee of being-in-the-world in exactly the same way as a photograph. Strange though it may be to say, on the level of environmental interaction, to be photographed may find analogy in other forms of waste-creation – a marking of territory that carries with it a certain exposure that can only be produced by the act of existing. As Boetzkes puts it: "Garbage stands as both signifier of an ecological condition and the materialization of that condition."[27] And perhaps so too for the image. Through her examination of garbage, Boetzkes theorizes a collapse of systems of value that would normally hold apart concepts like souls and plastic, or environment and excretion. Key to this compossibility is the concept of exposure, rethought by Boetzkes as a way to implicate ourselves in environmental catastrophe:

> The invitation is to think of the catastrophe that is happening to us (that we have created) as though it is us to whom it is happening ... We must imagine ourselves as other in order to experience what is happening. The other, both present and future, is also an imagined, nonnatural, precarious me/non-me. The ecological condition is not just a matter of delaying the return to a colonial, capitalist fiction of nature but of projecting an image of what is always already the case: that the exposure is already upon us now.[28]

But think about that in the context of photography, where exposure is the most basic operational function of the camera and thus the inherited condition of every image. Every picture is an exposure; every exposure an instantiation of the victory of image culture, a stolen soul that commemorates consumption by the camera in ways aligned with that of ecological harvest and waste.

Importantly, when I critique the deferral to the authority of images, I do not simply mean images of me. Instead, I mean the ideological system in which images hold this kind of environmental power over systems of relation. Lacan said it first – that self-image alienates the self from itself[29] – but Boetzkes provides a way to update this theory for a digital time where it is the body that is wasted in transactional interactions – the body photographed, or that of the Earth: Gaia herself.[30] Not the birth of self-reflexivity out of the recognition of oneself as other, but the othering of self, born from a deferral to the image as authority on appearances. Stolen souls and plastic Gaia. Thus, to reconfigure relations is key – and one reason why I admire Boetzkes's thought so much is that she sees in garbage (or that which has been garbaged) a certain plasticity whereby it is not just wasted energy but vibrant as a guarantee of a certain form of life. She calls it "mana":

> Waste might be viewed as a kind of mana, the transgressive energies galvanized by collective beliefs and enlisted through ritual to produce social transformation ... Like mana, the power of waste lies as much in its ideological and economic framing as in the animate vibrancy of its ontological reality.[31]

For me, mana in this context is about stolen souls, images turned into energy and redistributed or rechanneled into neoliberal systems of exploitation. Of course souls can be stolen – at least in a metaphoric way. But metaphors need to be taken seriously, and the vampiric economies of emotional engagement in which neoliberal life unfolds is nothing if not a literal farmyard for affective capital. To complement the idea that photographs steal souls, the idea of images as energetic (bodily) excretions.

## Ecopoetics of Blur

The end point here will be very unsatisfying. Photographs do steal souls, but in order to get them back I must think against the grain of focused vision. The firm boundaries of articulated vision simply uphold outdated categories of thought, they deprive existence of creativity, of mana. Boetzkes writes: "In order to think toward Gaia, we must rather deanimate modern thinking," and I think she's right for more than only environmental questions.[32] The question of photography is a symbolic addendum to Boetzkes's analysis, suggesting that the over-articulation of any environment (natural or image-based) requires a creative intervention in order to revive the possibilities of spirited engagement.

It could be seen as a gambit, embracing the idea that cameras actually provide a sense of being seen – exactly not the colonial vision machine of Virilio's imagination, but rather a plastic soulfulness that is powerful precisely because it doesn't care if a soul is real or not. If I have no soul and a camera steals it anyway, then indeed the image manufactures the reality in which I live with great expertise. Or better – with a soulfulness that charges the world with a sense of immediacy it might not otherwise have. But that only works if one is willing to wager the soul on an image.

To think this more ecologically would be to see it as simply as being-in-the-world: if cameras manufacture this sense of being soulfully seen, then I need to behave such that the camera knows I see it and am aware of the transaction it proposes. There is something sacrificial to my relationship to the camera but also something curious: I can see it differently than it sees me, but the camera – not me – holds the power of documentation that sets the dominant context. Consequently, if I want to participate in this economy of images, if I am to be properly ecological about refashioning my relationship to the camera, my return gaze needs to also be an invitation (or maybe just a purposeful marking of my position in the dynamic).

To then return to the exercise that catalysed this chapter would be to suggest that Cross-eyed visions, as a participatory project, proposes an alternate energy to the photographic apparatus – one not bound to focused vision but to the energy of the gaze, the "mana" of the system, which can only really come out when it refuses to be instantly recuperated by the logic of focused vision. Cross-eyed visions tries to give soul back to the camera, allowing it to see something it cannot understand, and thus an opportunity to increase and expand its own awareness of the differences within the world it (the camera) inhabits. It does it by wasting focus, by insisting on wasted focus as an object of focused vision, by proposing thus that focused vision reconsider its hegemony of precision ideology and consider the possibility of blur. An **ecopoetics of blur** engages and recreates the image apparatus as a relational device, giving the camera the power to not resolve nuance, but rather to hold space for what it itself cannot actually see – the world that appears in two ways at once.

# 2

# Necro-Reflectivity

**Exercise 2: Take a Mirror for a Walk**

**Framing statement:** The French writer and literary critic Stendhal (Marie-Henri Beyle) once asserted that "the novel is a mirror one takes for a walk," which he meant as a critique of the ways in which literature is tied to the (self-reflective) experience of author and reader.[1] In this, there is also a critique of everyday life, which is connected no less than literature to the fictions sustained every time we look into the mirror. It's an artist's dream – and sometimes nightmare – the simple observation that reality is bound to the mirrors we use to construct it, or better, to make sure we ourselves are part of the realities we see around us. In (Lacanian) psychoanalysis, we see ourselves in the mirror, therefore we exist – and yet such an existence is both optically and psychologically tainted (formed through the fantasies we build about the selves we see).[2] In communications, we represent ourselves (through images), therefore we exist – our very existence dependent on an ability to sustain the interest of others in the images we put forward. Clicks and likes and followers and shares are the new feedback mechanisms through which we construct (real) fantasies of who we imagine ourselves to be.

In some ways, then, our own fictions of ourselves always walk along the path beside us – and all the better when they are mirrors too – friends who might be imaginary but which nevertheless reflect a side of the world we know and trust. But there is also an opportunity here to take seriously Stendhal's suggestion that something different from "regular" life happens when we approach such a relationship artistically –to walk with our mirrors figuratively and literally.

**Guidelines:** This project asks what it looks like when one "walks a mirror" most literally. In order to participate, simply take a mirror for a walk. This might be the secret mirror in a shoulder bag, a mirror brought and placed in a public location, or the bathroom mirror in an arbitrary location – but in all instances it is bound to be a mirror that is in some way familiar. (Is it not the same self that appears in each mirror, after all?) Document your process and take a picture at the end.

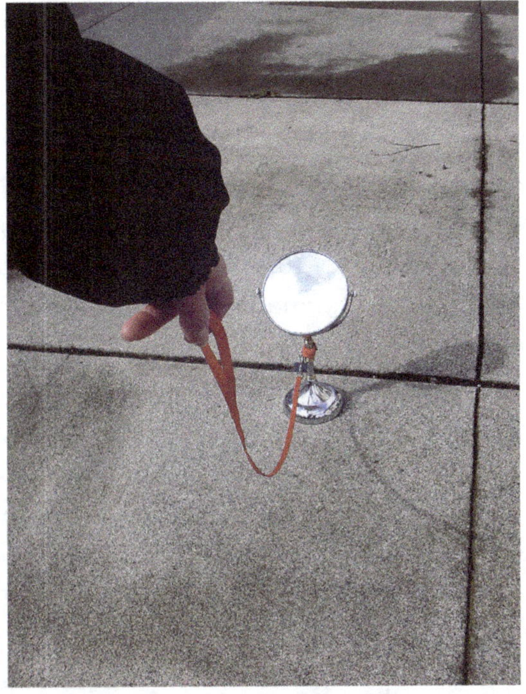

Figure 2.  Andrew Wille, *To Walk a Mirror*, photograph, 2011

## To Walk a Mirror

On a sidewalk rests a mirror, bound to a hand by a thin red leash. It's a small, round mirror on a stand; after a bit of digging for details, Amazon specifies that it's a tabletop make-up mirror. The difference is, perhaps, important – a mirror made exactly for the purposes of composing a face in private, here brought out into a public world. Not a pet, then, though at first it seems like it might be. The hand holds the leash in a way that is almost tender. The mirror looks back – up – in a way that is almost expecting, anticipating. Almost anthropomorphic.

In the mirror, though, is not a face. In the mirror is the sky – juxtaposed against the concrete of urban transit. In its simplest interpretation this is the sidewalk looking at itself, imaging itself as sky only to realize it is already the transit horizon of the urban imagination. Self-realized urban delusions of freedom. But on closer inspection, this is – if it is anything – a leashed freedom, bound as it is to the hand of someone standing to the side. An elegant solution that proposes a fantasy universe in which sidewalks are self-reflective and humans actually control their own movements through scripted city space. It's a lie, of course, like any reflection. Sidewalks exist to shuttle people between points, just as urban architecture is made to keep bodies in efficient motion, stopping only when needed to keep external flows in check. The Situationists made a big deal of this kind of social scripting, but despite their critique, it's never really gone away.[3] Maybe it's because we like it – stop signs mean we don't have to look at each other except to note who arrived first; traffic lights allow us to absent-mindedly follow a system of regulation instead of negotiating our way past fellow people. In fact, it often feels rude to make eye contact while waiting at a traffic light. It's all designed to keep us apart from each other. No loitering.

But what if the Situationists had it wrong? What if really this kind of urban scripting can be so effective not because of some strange power it has to control behaviour but just because I'm lazy and like it? What if Lacan was wrong too, and the mirror wasn't the surface that alienates me from myself but instead what lets me retreat from the pressures of living? Not an image; a mask. What if the mirror actually walks me? Look at this mirror, patiently waiting for the human to make the next move. There is no uncertainty in its gaze; only the confidence of a technologically reflected imagination. I might start by taking a mirror for a walk, but in the end the walk I pursue belongs to the mirror.

## The Death of Reflection

The project is a total set-up. The idea that I might take my reflection for a walk assumes that I am the operating agent and the reflection my faithful companion. It's the promise of documentary media, but it is a total lie, or at least a partial lie, a mediated half-truth that definitely doesn't walk itself. Read reflection, instead, as a process of animation. Not a living document of a living world but a dead moment seen in real time.

Until further notice, then, consider the possibility that reflection is best understood as a death dealer, waiting in the shadows to be reanimated as a counterpoint to an increasingly accelerated lifestyle. As a principal and as a phenomenon, reflection is not to be trusted and perhaps only for that reason is still interesting. Phantom images of a world I wish to be part of, reflection is instead a guarantee of my exclusion. Thus I must find ways to speak back to my reflection if I am to survive – or at least I must develop a relationship with it – a relationship premised not on healthy dialogue, but rather on an interplay of materiality and simulacrum.

But the fact of the matter – if I am to pursue the metaphor – is that, until further notice, I am dead too – living on a haunted planet in a present and future made sustainable only by the power of hope, and more realistically grief. I am not unlike my reflection except that my reflection must outlive me if it is to survive – and it must develop a relationship with those around me as carriers of its material yet simulacral relevance. It might seem complicated, but it's actually really easy: it's just social media as a form of necro-reflectivity.

Necro-reflectivity? Isn't that what happens when only vampires actually see themselves in the mirror – or when images outlive the bodies they pretended to represent and now reanimate a spirit all their own? There are two sides to any reflection (the image and the imagination); this just reverses the location of each to insist that I am the reflection of my image and not the other way around. My mirrors finally confess that I was just there to help them imagine. Actually I am not actually there at all: ambiguous, abstract, ephemeral. But there is something beautiful about this kind of absence: while it fails to answer the questions of presence it provides a framework for the plausible manifestation of whatever else one might imagine.

I engage with the world visually (and I assume the same for most others), but the one thing that I have no direct visual reference point for is myself, especially my face. I know myself (in this apperceptive way) only in reflection and in image. I stare at the mirror and I see ... myself as I can never actually know myself. Absent.

Nothing is a placeholder for anything. Conscience with creativity. Maybe. The endgame of **Walking a Mirror** is thus not the affirmative insistence on appearances but just the opposite, a precarity of reflection now understood as the phantom image of identity.

## Reflection after the Death of Reflection

It's a strange world that this meditation renders – a reflection after the death of reflection, as if to imagine that death could be self-reflexive or that it could, at least, persist in some strange way in excess of itself. A strange encounter, what the poet Joyelle McSweeney calls a form of endtime aesthetics that can be so powerful because it admits to no exclusions – powerfully proximate as only the dead can be. Not just an embodied proximity – maybe more like disembodied proximity, like trauma or haunting or fatigue when the body is so close to itself as to disassociate from the world itself.[4] It's an extended – endgames – version of Peter Slotdisjk's concept of "critical proximity" as an argument against the emphasis on rational living.[5] Instead, Sloterdijk and McSweeney both prioritize those moments that would be entirely uncapturable by the camera if it were not for the fact that we are wizening up to the deceit of the image and starting to see the technological death mask for what it really is. There are some things that cameras don't see. Those are the only things worth taking pictures of. All the others just prove the death of the world.

## The Provocation

What would happen if we took as a challenge the constitution of a strange world where Joyelle McSweeney was the sequel to Peter Sloterdijk and endtimes living was seen not only as a consequence of environmental catastrophe but also as the new (forthcoming) existential condition of thought in the first place? And then, what would happen if we tried to think of photography from this perspective – from a place of lived catastrophe rather than one of privileged distance?

## The Short Form

**Joyelle McSweeney** is an American poet and the star of this juxtaposition, a thinker that moves me with her theory of the "necropastoral" as a reinvention of aesthetic engagement after the end of the world.[6] It's a thesis that can be so fitting for this historical moment because it is grown exactly out of a conscience of ecological end times and an insistence on the importance of continuing to covet what McSweeney calls "strange encounters" that can be animating – even after the end of the world – because they understand themselves as already belonging to a post-catastrophe imagination.[7] The necropastoral is the (hopefully creative) romanticization of ourselves as already dead.

**Peter Sloterdijk** is a German philosopher that I love best for his theories of philosophical action, which he constitutes through reference to the Greek figure of Diogenes as an embodied counterpoint to Socrates, Plato, and Aristotle – in other words, an alternative history of Western philosophy.[8] Sloterdijk refuses the "critical distance" so lauded by reasonable rationalism in favour of what he calls "critical proximity" to questions that matter.[9] He also calls this kynicism,[10] in essence a version of what has been radicalized and popularized in recent years by thinkers like Donna Haraway as a form of "staying with the trouble" rather than trying to understand it (trouble) from the outside.[11] In a sense, the idea is to accept one's status as part of the problem, proximate to and implicated in, and to work from the inside towards substantive social or philosophical change.

What I'm proposing, then, is to consider the idea of McSweeney as a twenty-first-century sequel to Sloterdijk – zombie Sloterdijk reanimated in the spirit of dead mirrors and living reflections, sustained by the power of persistent creative intervention. Forget kynicism as an intervention into the canon of enlightenment philosophy (or any form of salvational modernism) and instead read philosophical action as the necropastoral condition of endtimes living.

## Homeopathic Proximity

Forget critical distance (or just take a picture). The idea that one might best understand a situation by being detached from it runs a serious risk of informatic elitism and inhuman(e) conscience. It is definitely not how I create my own intellectual stakes: I care most about the things that I am closest to. But being part of something in a high-stakes way comes with a certain kind of responsibility. At least a sense of implication, a stake in the question, an experimental proximity. It seems like it should be a philosophical prerequisite to any kind of intellectual pretence. In short, what is needed is an allegiance to the performative, something provided by no one better than Peter Sloterdijk, whose critique of philosophy works against enlightenment thinking by giving permission to be defiant towards forms of logic that prioritize detached (usually privileged) analysis: "If things have become too close for comfort for us, a critique must arise that expresses this discomfort. It is not a matter of proper distance but of proper proximity."[12] Sloterdijk refuses the idea that detached reason is possible, that philosophy could have no lived stakes and could thus be a purely speculative practice. He calls it kynicism, tracing the origins of this form of thought to the Greek philosopher Diogenes:

> In *kynismos* a kind of argumentation was discovered that, to the present day, respectable thinking does not know how to deal with. Is it not crude and grotesque to pick one's nose while Socrates exorcises his demon and speaks of the divine soul? Can it be called anything other than vulgar when Diogenes lets a fart fly against the Platonic theory of ideas – or is fartiness itself one of the ideas God discharged from his meditation on the genesis of the cosmos?[13]

More recently, Sloterdijk pushes this insistence on the bodily grounds of thought into the realm of the homeopathic.[14] I want to think this question for the photograph too –

acknowledging that the homeopathic is a counter-intuitive notion for the simulacral logic of the image, but one that eloquently anchors the theatrical and the reflective as twin axes of photographic thought. In some ways this might be exactly what's at stake in the question of the image – a futile attempt to objectify myself in the name of proving that I exist (in a certain way, or perhaps at all). No document, no existence. Certainly that's the twenty-first-century version of informatic living in which the passport picture holds border authority in a way a body never could. But maybe it's more than that too. Maybe it's indicative of an ideological conflation of political and philosophical being. Maybe the problem really is existential, or more specifically a twenty-first-century short-circuiting of the existential question of death and suicide, the foundational question that was so unavoidable to Camus and many others. But where Camus opted against suicidal being ("I rebel therefore we exist"[15]), living kynically (with self-reflexive proximity) after the end of the world involves just the opposite: accepting the irony that lived presence only materializes as a stake in the format of postmortem documentation. I might, after all, live on in data after my body has been obliterated by the environmental ecosystem that I have helped to create. My photographs will outlive me.

The solution is not to understand the photograph as rationally distant but as homeopathic – that is, as a postmortem proximity. To paraphrase Sloterdijk is to follow his invocation of Samuel Hahnemann's "principle of effective remedy" by which "if one is to be a doctor, one's body must become the first site of experimentation."[16] As Sloterdijk puts it: "the concept of self-experiment stems from this reflection: if you intend to be a doctor, you must try to become a laboratory animal."[17] The same seems intuitively true for photography. To contextualize kynicism in this way is to understand performativity philosophically – embodied experimentation as the basis for social existence. The photographic self-portrait is the first existential gesture, a distancing of oneself from oneself by means of hyper-proximity. In this, the self-portrait is homeopathic.

Sloterdijk suggests that "It is characteristic of one type of aesthetic theory that it never discusses a phenomenon without incorporating some element of what is being discussed into the discourse itself."[18] In turn, I refuse the idea that speculation is abstract or that philosophy should seek answers applicable to everyone in the same ways. I refuse objectivity, even in – or perhaps especially in – a self-portrait. I refuse ontology, especially in the sense of a philosophical positionality that might exist without a subject. It might be a precarious position for a photographer to occupy, given that the premise of photography is somehow related to the evidencing of impartial truths. But, I believe, that in the conversation about the photograph, the stakes of the philosophical question take on new intensity.

But there is also something else at play in the homeopathic, a simulacral logic through which the cure is not redemptive but excessive. "Like cures like."[19] So too with the photograph – the perfect solution to a self that is alienated from itself by self-image is a self-portrait which has the potential to creatively multiply the stakes of identity and thus entirely destroy the power of alienation by making it the coveted and theatrical norm rather than a default existential condition. Homeopathic existentialism.

## Zombie Existentialism

Let's move towards coveting theatrical norms. It is the right thing to do, not least because it seems that theatre – and by extension, photography – may have always had its roots in a meditation on death.[20] A contemplation of dead moments captured such that they might die again and again – a Promethean spectacle, sentenced each night to have his liver eaten by vultures, just to regrow it again (and again and again) in the morning. What a photograph represents is a different kind of time. Not instantaneous but recursive; not the static presentation of a validated memory but an occult procedure through which a dead moment is dialogically reborn through the act of ... looking. And if we live in a time operationalized by the technical ideology of Arthur Kroker's "will to technology," this is to say also that we live under the sign of photographic logic – what presents itself first as the logic of high-resolution, hyper-focused, unbiased information, but is in reality just the opposite – a zombie existentialism through which dead signs circulate at the speed of life.[21]

This may seem counterintuitive, since it is not the version of linear time that is used to operationalize productivity. It is something more like what Joyelle McSweeney calls "bug time," or a "chitinous necropastoral hypertime against the future" noting that non-anthropocentric time (in this case bug time – there is no reason to think that all non-anthropocentric modes of engagement would be similar) proceeds not only with a different rhythm but one that fundamentally dissonates with that of the human.[22] Bugs simply don't covet self-improvement or progress for their own sake in the ways of the human. They live and die much too quickly to learn and adapt at a scale of human activity. But – and this is the important part – they don't have to. Bugs have evolution on their side, genetic evolutionary speed as the result of fast living. McSweeney's intuition is to ask what kind of interventions into poetry or literature might be provided by this articulation of evolutionary speed ramping. Her conclusion is resonantly postmodern – proliferation rather than succession – one evolves a practice most rapidly by dying, not by building. "Death shits evolution," says McSweeney, "evolution is its waste product."[23] And for McSweeney, as death shits evolution, so too do bodies excrete language.[24]

Now this is, of course, partly metaphoric (the literary part) and partly quite literal (the bug part). But what if we collapsed that distinction for a moment and thought homeopathically? What does homeopathy look like when seen with post-apocalyptic eyes, eyes that see shit instead of images? This is not disaster tourism, an ideological artefact of minds that consider themselves safely alive. This, instead, is the necropastoral, a form of zombie existentialism in which being dead already is no argument against the fact that I wake up today like any other. Or perhaps exactly not like any other. Like today. I wake up today like today. Already dead. That is, I die into being – anamnesis, only in a much more excretory way. Not that version of consciousness where I forget myself forward, remembering the future as I move in its direction. Instead simply following the trail of shit and realizing that if I want to change the trajectory that it maps out that I need to eat different foods, take different pictures, excrete (or just live) differently.

No amount of thinking will save us from the images we have already taken. Their imagination has already been set in motion – that's the way technical ideology works: as a script. To change this future it is not enough to think about it differently; it is necessary to take different images, and in so doing begin to (theatrically) create different possible futures. Put differently, it might be ethology, or entomology, or aphotography – as a speculative homeopathic proposition: if one is to treat oneself as the first site of experimentation (as Sloterdijk suggests), and if the topic up for engagement is bug time, or zombies, or photography, or whatever, then the "effective remedy" isn't really a remedy but an excessive – which is to say dramatic – existential repositioning. This version of the necropastoral is not an invocation of excess as a romantic superfluidity of identity but as shit. Images as shit. The camera excretes me (the mirror too) – I am its waste product, not its *raison d'être*. Despite the fact that it sounds crass to put it so bluntly, zombie existentialism is self as image shit. Exactly against representational thinking. Photography is scripture. Corpse time is kynical.

## Nihilist Ecopoetics

Reject technicity, at least in its current form, even at the expense of the verifiable and the true. These are not functional categories anyway, relying already on a refusal of the intuition, the imagination, multiplicity, complexity, and anything ambiguous.

And the idea of the self as an after-effect of the image is not as depressing as it sounds. It's really just an acknowledgment that life unfolds within an ecosystem dominated by images. That is, images in that particularly technical form that we have come to assume they deserve – with its ideological extensions in the form of information, informatics, visualization, and data. The assertion of technological ubiquity is so self-evident that it is not even radical anymore; the radical part comes from thinking about it as an ecosystem, since that naturalizes the technical as an ecopoetic companion to contemporary living. The lie of objectivity is that distance saves us from the technical domination of the image. What is needed, instead, is a hyper-subjectivity that enables a simple sense of defeat. Simply look at it from *your own* perspective – and realize what will never translate from your images to others. Too often we think about images as objects rather than ideological catalysts; this is a mistake. Homeopathy applied to the technological (or photographic) conscience is actually rather simple – it's not about what the technology is or does; it's about what happens at that moment when we engage with it. And in this case we lose. McSweeney (thinking about the literary rather than the photographic) eloquently calls it the "loser occult": Loser occult is a rejection of any concept of literature still trying to worship at that old altar of patrilineal, of literary inheritance."[25] It is occult because it is not an argument; instead what McSweeney knows so well is that refusal is a gesture of incantation: refusal has the power to be a form of manifest illogic with the power to generate alternate ways of imagining. It is an occultation, a defiance that bends the logic of inheritance in different ways. "The loser occult gnaws that edifice down, hangs out in the rubble huffing, hallucinating, gossiping, making out, wasting time, confecting new and obscene humid and nonhumanoid forms."[26]

But think about that in the context of photography. No less a dominant form of logic than literature, perhaps even more so for its (photography's) illicit affiliation with science. What would it mean to reject images that profess faith in the reality they inherit? Would it not be a rejection of the real itself – in exactly those categorical, hierarchical, patrilineal, and inherited ways? To instead *make* images that represent differently, and thus set into motion different versions of reality. It is decidedly *not* to supplant one version of the real with another (it's not better – it's still just reality). Instead, this act can be so crucial not because of its argument but because of its defiance. I think of Jean Baudrillard who eloquently argued that reality dies through excess, not through argumentation.[27] He's right – and McSweeney too – and all the others, everyone, define your realities such that any singular reality collapses under the weight of difference and thus just gets out of the way. It's the kind of thinking that can only happen when there is nothing left at stake, of course – that's why this whole meditation happens under the shadow of existentialism. For if the world is indeed already over, then that's that. It's not a revolution; it's simply acknowledging the failure of the project of virtuosic representation and refusing technical redemption in the name of messy community.

The good news is that the argument is an alibi – that is, there is nothing to learn here. The proposition is entirely self-fulfilling since it's the way the image operates already. That is, there is no moral to this story, no lesson to be learned, no different way I am proposing for how to think about pictures. It's all a scam, a perfectly rendered technological sham, Morel's island on which I propagate myself through dead narratives as a basic mode of sociality.[28]

## Necro-Reflectivity

The idea of siding with the dead might seem counter-intuitive, but it's not – it's actually just the required negligence of the dominant system of reflective thought. That is, there is a social imperative to seem alive, to perform attentiveness, to feign caring – and these manifest most explicitly at moments of social documentation – epitomized perfectly by the camera. But it's not that hard to side with the dead. I follow McSweeney's wisdom when she says: "It's not that difficult to interact with the dead. Everyone who is dead is available. Every dead letter, every dead art form, every dead Kennedy, every dead idea."[29]

Every dead self.

The encounter between a self and its image has always been strange – and it's no different for the encounter between me and myself, or, I assume, any other and their own selves too. For me, it mimics the ways McSweeney describes her necropastoral as a series of "strange meetings" that "may not ever solidify into 'outcomes'":

> [W]e never know what the "outcome" is, the "outcome" never stops happening, the outcome can only be damage, the outcome sometimes happens backwards, has irrational retrospective events, reinserts itself in the field, tears the mucous membrane of the field, the outcome is anachronistic, reedited, happens at different speeds, we can't link the cause to the effect because we reject the ideological primacy of the "cause" and because we are interested in illicitly generating so very very very very very many unearned and exorbitant effects.[30]

The endgame of this mode of necropastoral thought is, for McSweeney, the ambition to be "derelict," a beautiful conclusion for the ways it simply refuses to participate in the economy of reflective performance.[31]

To loop back to the exercise from which this chapter unfolds, I might suggest that To Walk a Mirror, as a participatory photography project, has the potential to be the kind of derelict endeavour McSweeney proposes; refusing the mirror as a screen on the wall and insisting on the mirror as an object. It is to drag a mirror through the dirt, even if it gets my image dirty – or maybe especially because it gets my image dirty. How else? Dirty images are not easy to come by, nor the self-reflections they are capable of engendering. Against the ideology of critical distance, a conscientious attempt to implicate oneself in the relational presence of images. **Necro-reflectivity** is a strategically performative use of the camera to re-cast reflective relationships between a dying world and a self already dead by existential association.

# 3

# Smash Metaphysics

**Exercise 3: Smash Something and Take Its Picture**

**Framing statement:** In 1913 Marcel Duchamp invented the idea of the readymade, a precursor to photography in the sense that Duchamp simply took things that already existed – a urinal, a shovel, a bicycle wheel – and treated them as objects for artistic display.[1] Understandably, not everyone saw the artistic element of these everyday items. One might equally wonder how any photographic image might claim to be a work of art, being as they tend to be replications of a world that already exists: readymades in exactly Duchamp's sense. There is nothing less creative than a photograph.

A few years later, Duchamp proposed what he called an "art coefficient" that was meant to help articulate the difference between an artist's intention and a viewer's encounter of a work.[2] To help collapse this distance, he suggested the idea of the "readymade aided," an everyday object with an explicit intervention (a text, a red dot, a placement in a gallery) that could serve to anchor the intentionality of the work. Such an idea mashes together the real and the artistic through an act of collapse – a questioning of the (function of the) real that makes it artistic, and an explicit action within the artistic imagination that promises a certain lived reality of encounter. In this sense, a readymade is simply an intention attached to an object and then made public – the performance of an idea of art that is imposed onto an object in ways both honorific and violent. Readymades smash the distinctions between life and art – and more importantly, those between art and life.

**Guidelines:** This project takes literally the idea of breaking the boundaries between life and art. In order to participate, find (or create) a readymade and smash it. Realize that, whatever the object you select, you are smashing something that is already a work of art (because you selected it) and that your act of smashing creates a work of art as well. Intention meets intervention. Document your process and take a picture at the end.

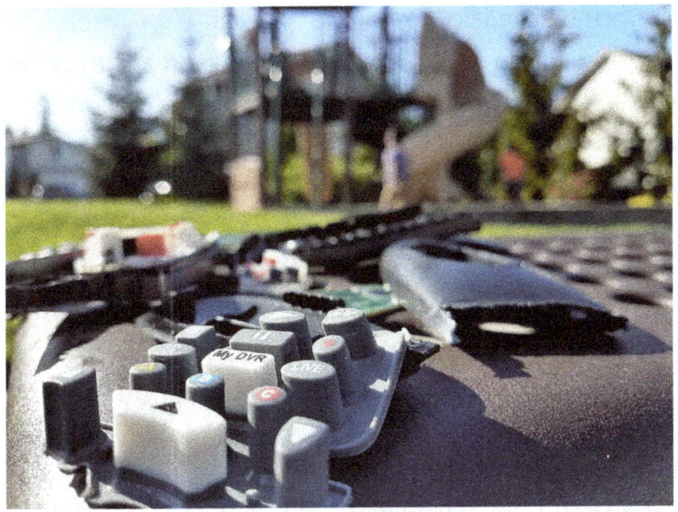

Figure 3. Melissa Gueiros, *Smash*, photograph, 2017

## Smash

On a bench beside a playground sits a broken remote control
or console handset of some sort, recognizable for the buttons
and text, though the details of brand and shape are harder to
place. The device has been torn apart, a half dozen discarded
pieces abandoned as litter or victims of game time frustration.
It's hard to know. The playground behind it is empty, though
a couple of blurry bodies give human presence to the scene.
It's the kind of juxtaposition that makes it clear we're seeing
a composed image – something purposeful, even cliché about
the arrangement of broken technology and playground. It

could be a found scenario, but it probably isn't; it is probably instead a provocation to think about the registers of digital and analogue play. But staged. Ironically staged, in portrait mode, though not perhaps exactly as one might expect.

The irony is not the juxtaposition between the broken game controller and the playground – the irony is that in its staging this picture reveals exactly the opposite of its apparent intent. Not a provocation to smash technologies, but rather a smooth conforming to the very logic of technological provocation. Staged provocation. A simulation. It only seems like a portrait of a lonely and broken piece of technology. Despite the broken console, it is a happy picture – perhaps a Hallmark moment when the broken device brings into focus options for more analogue forms of play. Only that seems backwards, since the playground is out of focus; the broken console up close to the camera as though pleading for sympathy. I feel none. There is something very poised, maybe too poised, about this image.

It takes me a moment to figure out what is wrong; the image is aware of itself. This picture knows it's a picture – and shares that it has been made for me to look at. That's one of the effects of portrait mode, of course, an optical effect that insists on a technical, and thus inhuman, representation of the image. Humans don't see in portrait mode, though we do focus our eyes differently when looking at people and other objects. But a camera forces the issue – pre-focusing the human gaze and thus imposing upon the eyes and mind a certain, well, focus. So this image is a recording – the only thing in clear focus are the words "My DVR: LIVE" – a recording of a moment waiting to happen. Or better, a pre-recording, a promise constructed in order to pre-focus the gaze to the controls – broken for technology but smashed apart in such a way as to provoke a human into action.

Or to propose that we already have been called upon. This simulation hands us the remote control – it is My DVR: LIVE after all. Except that the controls have been broken and no matter how hard I press the buttons the future before me has already been pre-focused.

## After the Smash

I'm imagining a photograph of the world I live in, a world of climate crises, social and political injustices, and deep-seated elitisms but also one peppered with creative artistic ingenuity, accelerated technological development, and ideas that range from wacky to prophetic to moralizing to panicked to power-hungry to delusional. Such a photograph has no generalizable content (it would be a bit different for each person, I imagine), but it does have immanently particular form (growing from individual imaginations of personal context). No message, only punctuation – a thought object that implants itself with the power of crisis into my imagination. A *punctum* perhaps in that way that Roland Barthes described it as a rupture, this time psychic.[3] James Elkins likened this effect to that of a toothache: I see your toothache and it makes my teeth hurt too. Or perhaps Susan Sontag's metaphor of the camera as a "predatory weapon" is better, something that I feel ominously pointing my direction.[4] Or better still, Ariella Azoulay's proposal of the idea of a "phantom photograph" that haunts the imagination with its images – real or not, the haunting power of such images have material effects.[5] I cannot unsee my world; or perhaps more haunting still, I would not choose to unsee it.

Maybe it's strange to imagine a photograph that doesn't already have a visual subject – but I'm working off an intuition that tells me that photographs do more than document an external world. Or if they do document external worlds, they are still ones that make me feel a certain way – that resonate or speak or remind. Without that power an image would just be information. But this particular photograph that I am imagining – the photograph that, as near as I can tell, is a photograph of the end of the world, troubles me. And the most troubling part is that I imagine that it has already been taken – such is always already the nature of the photograph, after all. Maybe we're still waiting for the image to process, just as the world still goes on after its end, but also maybe that's not right (it's a rather old school analogy after all: images take no processing time anymore). So maybe it's actually just the opposite – maybe this image is actually so present in my mind because it is the image I see everywhere I look: on Instagram, Facebook, chats and messages and discords, on my phone, on your phone. Not a photograph that has already been taken but one that sticks on repeat, the only photograph that it is still possible to take. Maybe every picture is exactly a picture of the end of the world? Something smashed. Maybe something big, maybe something small.

This would not be just another metaphor of photographic violence, or maybe it would be with the caveat that metaphors should be taken more seriously. The role of the poetic is not to safely evoke but to double. The power and beauty of metaphors is that they are literally two things at once, both themselves and something else that is nonetheless still part of what they are too. Metaphors – taken literally – are entangled concepts that add dimensionality to the informatic by insisting on contexts in which things are also other things. Seen in this way, to smash something for the sake of an image is a chance to think about larger complexities of disaster and how to build and mitigate already existing relationships with a troubled world. And to smash something small is a symbolic action that situates a photographer within the matrix of disaster, owning a part in this future we have built – together.

Smash metaphysics? Isn't that what happens when we choose self-implication over detached representation, the dramatic over the documentary? If I accept that I am complicit in anthropocentric logic then there is no objective escape route – photographic or otherwise. Every photograph a subjective document in some unusual way. And to refuse the conceit of objectivity is also to smash metaphysics – to refuse the idea that the world proceeds and survives us and to instead recon with human intervention and impact. Read smash metaphysics then not as a category of metaphysical thinking but as an imperative that is built into the very foundation of technological engagement. The endgame of **Smash** is not the cathartic human release that destroys a machine; it is awareness of the irony through which the machine recaptures its own destruction as a simulation of human hope.

# How to Greet the Death of the Future

Photographs have never been about archiving the past; they have always been about scripting the future. The documentary myth of the picture is a lie; and this lie is where its power as a medium comes from. Framing the past in order to predelict the future. The first predictive algorithm, what the philosopher Margret Grebowicz eloquently refers to as the "terraforming" power of the image.[6] It's a more nuanced and socially engaged version of Roland Barthes's eloquent insistence on the relationship between photography and death.[7] For Barthes, human death is the ultimate question of the future – and the camera a time travel device that poetically leverages one temporality (the technical) against another (the affective, or human). But in the twenty-first century the death of the future is already well integrated in the haunted (anthropocenic) present and something a bit more material is needed: a strategy for cultivating relationships with a future already simulated.

## The Provocation

What if human destruction of the planet was considered as something other than a technical and environmental disaster – perhaps a kind of perverse accomplishment? A natural effect of human impact rather than a mistake – perhaps intentional in ways we might not want to admit, perhaps even weirdly artistic in some kind of nihilist way? Might this be a world in which Margret Grebowicz's strategies for cultivating post-human relationships stood as the inheritor of Roland Barthes's assertion that photography owes its debt to the dramatic history of theatre and not, as is more generally thought, to the representational history of painting? And then what would happen if we tried to think of photography from this perspective – not as an archive of the natural world but as a dramatic production of futurity?

## The Short Form

**Margret Grebowicz** is a Polish philosopher and the star of this juxtaposition, a thinker that inspires me with her ability to build philosophical relationships: with technology, natural parks, whales, mountain climbing, and more. For me, Grebowicz is a thinker of relationality, and one who understands something that philosophy and photography share – the idea that when one builds a relationship with one's subject, the stakes of engagement increase. In photography, one seeks to "do well by" one's subject (making them look as good – or better – than they do in real life); Grebowicz brings this same ambition to philosophy, proposing the task of engagement as one of "greeting" ideas[8] such as to create what she calls "the collectivity to come."[9] That is, what Grebowicz inspires is an understanding of philosophy and photography alike, not as representations of the present or the past, but as manifestations of futurity: productions of hope and of relationships that require a conscientious understanding of ways to (non-anthropocentrically) greet the future.

**Roland Barthes** is a French poststructuralist thinker best known for his work on signs and his theory of the "death of the author."[10] For me, however, Barthes has always inspired a different way of thinking photography – as an affective practice devoted to imagining beyond the representational mechanics of the medium. His last book, *Camera Lucida*, meditates on the death of his mother and her presence in images, concluding that the camera is capable of creating deeply affective relationships because its central debt is not, as is generally assumed, to a history of painting but rather to that of theatre – creating images in ways that make possible different imaginations of the world.[11] For Barthes, the belief invested in the objective reality of technical reproduction is misplaced; instead, he encourages an understanding of the affective power of images to evoke tangential imaginations of different realities. Barthes refuses representation as the horizon of photography, insisting instead on the supererogatory details of the image that have the power to shape and inspire the imagination.[12]

What I'm proposing, then, is to consider the idea of Grebowicz as the inheritor of Barthes's relational legacy – a thinker who intuits the codes of theatricality inherent in social (or photographic) production and who understands philosophy (and photography) as a way to produce the individual, social, and political imagination. Forget the subjectivity of the image; this is photography as a "contractual mass mirage," a terraforming of the future imagination.[13]

## A World Seen with Closed Eyes

I am unwilling to let go of the invisible, even if it is exactly not the invisible that I see. The ruthless technical project of photographic representation does not convince me of the legitimacy of appearances; it makes me more suspicious. When I look at a picture, I am reminded that I do not see the picture – and in fact, in most instances, the picture doesn't see itself either. Just as I have no immediate visual presence to myself (except for the image mediated by mirrors and photographs), so too does the camera refuse its own existence in its capture of the world. It's not just a technical quirk; it's a defining characteristic of the photograph. A camera rarely appears in its own picture; pictures therefore pretend to be without self, though nothing could be further from the truth.

The most powerful distillation of this relationship – for me – has always been Roland Barthes's beautiful rendition of the picture in *Camera Lucida*, his last book and a meditation on photography mediated by the death of his mother. As the story goes, when his mother died Barthes searched his photographs of her, looking to find the familiar face of the woman he loved and remembered. But he didn't find her – he found only pictures – with one exception: a photograph of his mother as a child, standing in the garden. This picture – which Barthes referred to as "the Winter Garden photograph" – was never published. Barthes noted (accurately, I think) that for anyone else it would just be a picture of a child. But what made it special for him was exactly this non-transferable aspect that was his alone. In fact it was this element of non-transferability that made photography itself (as a medium) special; going somehow beyond the real to capture what was irreducible to the world and incommensurate with his own imagination. In a sense, this singular picture became the only one that mattered, the one from which Barthes claimed: "I therefore decided to derive all Photography (its nature) from the only photograph which assuredly existed for me (the Winter Garden image)."[14]

The reason I find this announcement so powerful is that its relationship is exactly counter to the enlightened and cynical response that insists representational media is not to be trusted. It is the opposite of René Magritte's famous painting of a pipe (subtitled with the words "this is not a pipe") – a painting that bears the title *The Treachery of Images* and thus becomes an admonishment for anyone who seeks authenticity in the image.[15] Barthes does just the opposite – basing his entire philosophy of photography on the unlikely possibility of representational authenticity, but not in a usual sense. The most present photograph – for Barthes – was one that documented a person he never knew in a time he had never witnessed – a representation of something, for him, entirely unrepresentable. Or, put differently, "in the Photograph, the power of authentication exceeds the power of representation."[16]

I understand this as the cognitive equivalent of the optical phenomenon of the "blind spot" – the spot in the human eye where we actually don't see because the optic nerve passes through the retina. It is a spot of darkness in human vision; but we don't see it. Instead, the brain fills in the gap and smooths over the image of the world. But I think of it as more than a technical operation; I think of it as a metaphor for the way all thought works. I think that something like this is what Barthes was also suggesting when he suggested that the photographic operation takes place in a spot called the "blind field" – a space that makes possible the suturing of temporal displacement in order to constitute impossible familiarities.[17] In Barthes's words, "ultimately – or at the limit – in order to see a photograph well, it is best to look away or close your eyes" and in so doing sacrifice that which is obvious (in the image) for that which it cultivates (in the heart and in the mind).[18]

This is not an insight – it is merely an attempt to place the camera as a weird affective catalyst for engagement rather than a tool for proving or understanding the world. A photograph is not a moment excerpted from time, it is literally temporally different – timed differently such as to create a second and surrogate timeline that smashes uncomfortably into the one I inhabit at any given moment. In some ways images that declare themselves artistic are the easiest to accept – they own their deceit and call it creativity. And I accept that trade. Harder for those images that pretend impartiality. Or for those that confront us with different versions of our past, present, and future. A photograph is never a memory, says Barthes, "it actually blocks memory, quickly becomes a counter-memory."[19] Or better, a future.

## The Production of Hope

Authenticity is overrated, for the simple reason that it is a self-referential concept and thus risks losing track of itself in its own process of self-justification. Authenticity has no transferability; it calls itself into question at the moment it seeks to justify its self-evidence. But the problem isn't with authenticity, not really; it's with the attempt to provide justification for something that needs none. That which is self-evident requires no evidence; its authenticity is guaranteed. The inverse, however, is not as simple. The inherent gambit of evidence is to present itself as self-evident – part of an argument that justifies itself as authentic. But in so doing, evidence reveals its own precarity: justification is always a construction or an argument, never simply self-evident. I make it seem confusing on purpose, since I see this particular confusion as central to the metaphysical intervention of the camera.

A few years ago my wife ran the Boston Marathon, and before the race we did the tourist thing of visiting the finish line and walking around to see the set-up. It was exactly as one would expect, a large inflatable archway, ribbons, balloons, and banners around to appropriately define the event – and written in large letters on the ground in front of the finish line, the word "FINISH." But what struck me was that the words were written in a way that would be upside down to a runner crossing the line. The words were written for the camera – not for the people actually crossing the finish, but for the camera already on the other side, tasked with documenting the "actual" finish of the individual. In a sense the camera had already crossed the line, already finished, already accomplished what the runners were still trying to do – and thus already in a privileged position of framing the reality of each individual runner.[20] Photographs taken here are not documents from the past but already images from the future, waiting to be seen by a runner looking back at themselves. The present is captioned in advance.

I read my experience as a humble instance of what Margret Grebowicz, in her analysis of the future of national parks, calls "terraforming": a vision of the present manufactured for a particular future function.[21] Grebowicz's imagination is much bigger than my own, as is her object of study – wilderness theorized as a conceptualization of "environmental nostalgia" that preserves a human capacity to imagine the non-human. Grebowicz argues that national parks are not monuments to the natural past but cultivated sites designed to help manufacture an imagination of the future in which nature persists.[22] They are simulations (isn't the Anthropocene exactly the refusal of the nostalgic idea that there are parts of the planet untouched by human impact?); however, the point is not to get stuck in the messiness of what counts as real, but rather to recognize the functional role of simulation in the production of authenticity. The clearest sign of simulation is that there is no sign of simulation. In the case of my example, the photograph would look wrong if the words "FINISH" were written upside down. Signage inside parks often shows what is unmistakably a camera icon, indicating an upcoming photo opportunity, which, thereby becomes a photo necessity. At the same time, since this imaginary is one of wilderness, we tend to take our park photos in such a way as to exclude the other cares, and indeed any signs of the other people.[23] This is more than a simple technical observation, reducible to good photography or design. Like Grebowicz, I think the act of design will always betray an ideological predisposition, excluding or preserving certain artificialities of the image in ways that manufacture the future that the image is to occupy in the human imagination. Put more simply: pictures produce the future of national parks (or Boston finishes) – not by documenting them in the moment but by creating an ontological futurity. They exist to be seen after the fact, romanticized perhaps but in a way that is more relevant to the future than to the present they purport to capture. Photographs are not about memory. I think Grebowicz is correct to say that they are about the production of hope.[24]

Take a moment to let that sink in. The idea that photographs "terraform" the mind is significant – treating the mind as a landscape to be designed and cultivated, made habitable. A manufactured image that looks like reality but actually holds space for something quite different than the actual moment: a habitable imagination of a natural world that somehow resists human domination. Photography is a technology of simulation, complicit in the production of nature because of its ubiquity – not because of its veracity. Not documentation; prophecy. A photograph does not prove that I was somewhere at a given time. It acts as a resource for the possibility that I may be somewhere in the future where a moment of having-been may matter again. And that's why it doesn't matter if a photograph tells the truth or not, because at stake is not the self-evidence of a moment but a capacity to invest it with embodied futurity. Terraforming.

## Blowing Bubbles

Terraform the mind! Refashion thought in ways that deliver future hope. What's beautiful about the production of hope is that it demonstrates that hope can be produced. DIY hope. Perhaps it's as simple as taking a picture for posterity – thus preserving the presence of nature in a hope for the future. It has the potential to be tricky, though, since such a tactic, while succeeding at the level of an ontological imagination, risks failing at the level of relationships. That is, like so many iterations of the technical imagination, it effectively reinscribes a dominant narrative but does so through a performance of unrequited (and unreciprocated) affect. It risks becoming a failed love story; one in which the simulation doesn't love me back. And why should it? Nature doesn't care about the picture I took. It's not a reflection; it's just another landscaped fantasy. Photography is always, at least partly, scopophilic.

But maybe there is another form of terraforming (and another form of photography), one that isn't about manufacturing artificial hope but about producing dramatic relationships – events that can be staged and retain a sense of authenticity precisely because they own a curiosity of encounter? For isn't relationality the opposite of objectification, and isn't curiosity a marker of dialogic intent? Margret Grebowicz – in her book *Whale Song* – calls it a "refined form of greeting,"[25] and she sees it in certain exceptional moments of natural science, in particular in the compelling story of Ingrid Visser, an orca researcher who has invented a way to greet the whales she studies – by blowing bubbles: "Together with the orcas she has come to know well over the years, she has invented something, a form of greeting: when they see her boat, the orcas Visser knows immediately swim up to it, at which point she sticks her face in the water and blows bubbles. The orcas respond by blowing bubbles back."[26] For Grebowicz, a greeting is an activity that is performed together with mutual curiosity – and importantly without (yet) requiring actual meaning. Grebowicz sees the act of blowing bubbles both literally (as the greeting it is) and metaphorically (as a greeting applied to other situations): "The bubbles 'mean' nothing to either of them," yet the activity establishes a space of interaction.[27] In this interaction Grebowicz sees the possibility of "greetings for a companion species."[28]

But think about that in the context of photography. What would it mean to think of the camera as a companion species rather than as a human tool or device with no agency of its own? And then, what might it mean to attempt to "blow bubbles" at the camera, so to speak? That is, could a piece of technology be imagined in the same register of thought as a whale? I am not in any way trying to offend whales – I am suggesting an anthropomorphism of the camera, taking seriously Steven Shaviro's idea that "in order to counteract anthropocentricism, a certain cautious anthropomorphism may be required."[29] Only, I would advise against caution – humans are overrated, and anthropomorphism has the potential to be a valuable critical tool to the extent that it can be used to exactly refuse human exceptionalism. So yes, anthropomorphize cameras and whales too – provided one views the act as one of introduction, greeting, and curiosity rather than one that levies the demand that, in order to demonstrate intelligence, companions must "learn to make humanoid sounds."[30] Deeply inhuman, cameras make few sounds – the whirr of automatic focus, the long click of capture – but they might see bubbles. And they might even automatically configure themselves to catch and capture those bubbles such as to prove to us that they have seen them too – that those bubbles were not just a figment of the human imagination but a moment shared, at least, with the camera. A personal witness, a companion.

But if an image is the camera's act of blowing bubbles, how might a human respond, stage a greeting for the camera, create a world designed particularly and especially for the camera to see? It could be a national park photo moment or a Boston Marathon finish, except that this may be already implied in each and every image. If so, it is a declaration of complicity rather than a greeting. Something a bit different is needed: the construction of a scenario that is not redemptive to nor confirming of the human, but rather appreciative of the metaphysical intervention of the image itself. Something that serves no human purpose and can therefore salvage human curiosity.

## Smash Metaphysics

"The greeting is the purest form of interaction," says Grebowicz.[31] It's a geography of hope constructed by terraforming the mind such as to undercut human exceptionalism by blowing bubbles at the camera. It's intimate play time. It's a creation of conditions: "While intimacy can only ever take us by surprise, this imperative reminds us that we can – and indeed, we must – create the conditions for it to do so."[32] I suppose this would be the reverse side of terraforming; not me caught within the photographic imagination already scripted for me by others, but instead staging reality itself such as to create moments of encounter (with the camera) that would not have otherwise presented themselves.

And that's smash metaphysics. Think of it as a proposition – smash (as an imperative) metaphysics. It's an anti-metaphysics metaphysics: no prefabricated existential world waiting to be scientifically discovered, but rather a deeply dialogic companion world waiting to be engaged. In this version, it all starts with an attempt to stage a greeting for the camera – to create something explicitly designed for its gaze is to blow bubbles at the camera in a first gesture towards owning a place in the cultural manufacturing of (photographic) curiosity.

To return to the exercise that catalysed this chapter, Smash, as a participatory photographic project, initiates the awkward conversation about how photographs change the world – not only by documenting it but by implementing a staging process that tends to be naturalized: "a photograph is always invisible: it is not it that we see," says Barthes.[33] But photographs are also in fact a new layer of metaphysical filtration brought to the performance of everyday life. Photographs create a category of behaviour performed for the camera; we might think of it as posed and therefore artificial, but it's actually nothing of the sort. It is a production of hope through relational acts of anthropomorphic theatre – impacting the foundation of how we imagine the worlds we live in. Against the assumption of images as representation, a staging of affect as effect and an embracing of photography as a theatrical art. **Smash metaphysics** is an offering to the camera, a staged material intervention that makes clear its gesture was made for the camera and not actually for the world. Smash metaphysics as a performance of photography designed to disclose and amplify the dramatic potential of the image.

# 4

# Non-Choreography

**Exercise 4: Take a Picture of Someone with a Chair Upside-Down on Their Head**

**Framing statement:** In the novel *Au Plafond* (*On the Ceiling*) by the French writer Éric Chevillard, the main character wears a chair upside-down on his head – an absurdist gesture and a creative horizon from which the story unfolds.[1] In the story, the chair serves as a prosthetic to correct the character's poor posture. In the world outside of the book, such an action might be thought of as a way to engage with the world a little more creatively. This project is an homage to the character in Chevillard's story, expanded into a documentary of everyday life made to act, for a brief moment, in strange ways. Chevillard writes:

> To my knowledge, no one before me has worn a chair upside down on his head as I do, or, if so, only for short distances – but, at the same time, it would seem that no one has avoided it altogether, that is, that everyone has tried it at least once ... I'm the first to keep it up.[2]

To seriously consider the idea of wearing a chair on one's head one needs to move past the idea that chairs are designed only to be sat upon. In so doing, one also might realize that the regular design of the chair not only dictates how the chair itself is used – it dictates how we ourselves use it too. Taking Chevillard's story as its starting point, this project asks you to use the chair differently.

**Guidelines:** This project asks you to engage in using a chair differently. In order to participate, take a photograph of somebody wearing a chair upside-down on their head. Whether the chair is a hat, a performance prop, or something else, realize that in the process of staging this picture you have re-scripted the possible uses of the chair, and the possible methods for human interaction. Consider staging your intervention in a public location.

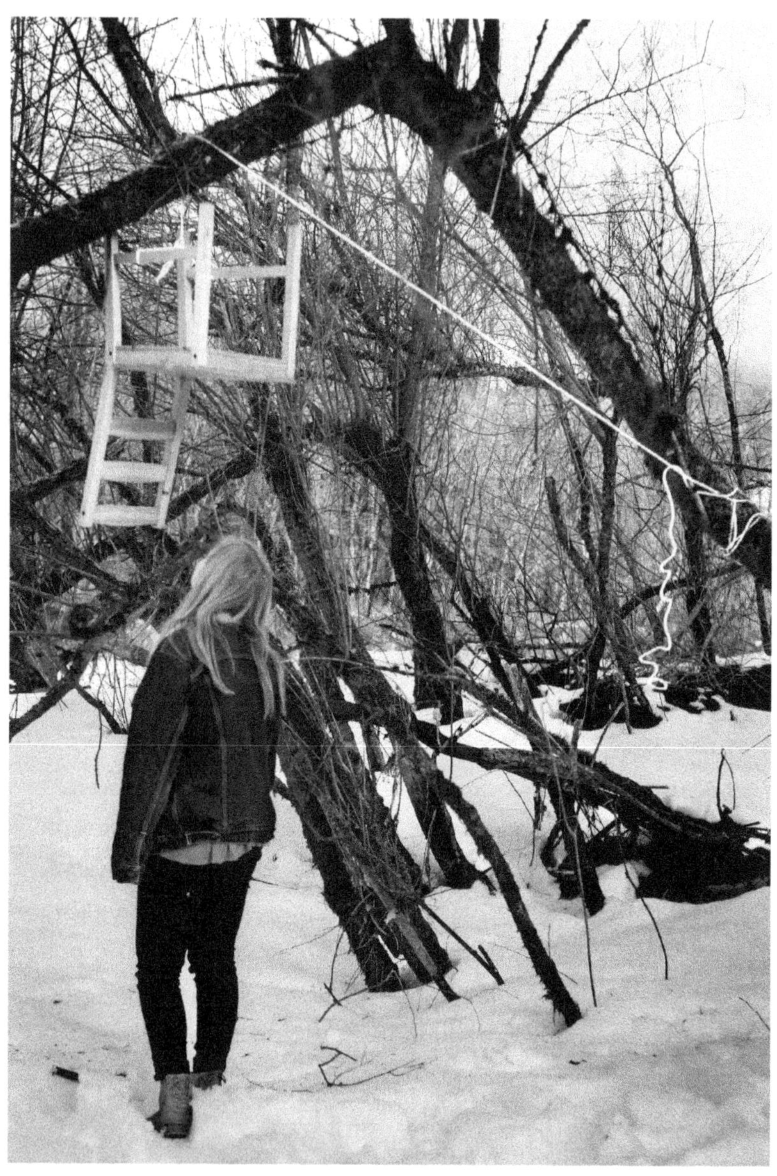

Figure 4.  Simon Perez, *On the Ceiling*, photograph, 2019

## On the Ceiling

A chair hangs from a tree in the forest, in the snow, upside down. There is a woman standing underneath it, looking up at the chair and away from me; she seems mostly beside the point. Instead, it's the chair that draws my attention – and hers too. But the chair also serves no immediate purpose, except perhaps to draw attention in exactly the way that it is doing – a different kind of script from what chairs usually perform, but one that nonetheless, in some strange speculative or metaphoric way, leaves me sitting on its surface.

I am aware in looking at the picture that it's a trap. Literally – like the chair is tied up over a tree branch in a way reminiscent of those Bugs Bunny cartoons where a box is propped up by a stick, tied to a string such that the box can be pulled to drop on anyone who dares within. Not just a trap, in other words, a caricature of a trap. But I notice that for me the chair reads as a box – not, for instance, an anvil or a piano. The chair is an invitation. The chair has a "within," a "strange encounter," a curiosity. It invites me to imagine an interaction.

This, then, is an unusual chair only for the reversal of perspective. Usually a chair invites me to sit on top of it: that is its script. Marshall McLuhan was a fan of this logic, by which technologies script responses from those who use them.[3] I walk into a room filled with chairs, and the first question I ask myself is which one I will sit on – not *if* I will sit or instead put the chair on my head. I obey the script of the chair quite faithfully, naturally – one might even say photographically: trusting in the instrumentalized myth of technological neutrality in which the chair itself doesn't make me sit (no hidden agenda to the chair!), I just happen to always do it of my own accord. Beautiful delusions of agency wrapped up in a convenient ergonomic accessory. I don't believe it on the best of days – the urge to sit is the chair's choreography and we are its dancers. It is almost Pavlovian.

This chair hung up in the tree, then, does something different, making clear that the picture is proposing a different kind of context. Something is happening. It is a strange encounter, but because it is photographed it becomes a bit more naturalized. I don't doubt that I see it. It is even, thus, plausible. Believable even, even if I don't quite know what it is that I am believing. But that's interesting – the idea that I could believe in a plausibility without knowing quite what it offers. It might be the definition of curiosity. Or the virtual. So maybe there's another option here, an invitation to vertigo. What if I tried to sit on this chair more directly, upside down, like a bat or an algorithm? Can one fall off an algorithm?


## A Chair Inside My Head


Two chairs sit opposite one another in an otherwise empty room. I am sitting in one of them, looking across the room at the other. I imagine what it would be like to be sitting in that chair instead. I imagine standing up and walking over to the other chair and sitting down on the other side of the room. I imagine looking back at myself sitting on the chair on the side of the room where I currently am. I decide to get up and walk over to the other chair to see if the experience matches my imagination. It's a bit odd, truth be told, since I was just imagining myself on that side of the room facing this way and now I find myself standing on this side of the room facing an imaginary self who is no longer there. Nonetheless I walk over to the other chair and sit down. It was just like I imagined. And so, here I am, sitting in a chair that I imagined myself sitting in just a moment ago, looking at a chair across the room where I sat only a short time before, imagining myself here where I am now. I repeat the experiment until I forget which chair I am actually sitting on and which one I am imagining.

This exercise is called the "2 chair experiment" and – according to occult consultant Robert Bruce – is a method for cultivating out-of-body experiences.[4] I am no authority on the paranormal, but what I do know is that playing this imagination game with oneself has the interesting effect of quickly confusing the boundaries between the real and the imaginary, such as to give some credence to the possibility of an imagination made real. It is a choreography designed to supplant itself, to undermine scripted action by triggering a state of performative vertigo. Worth noting is that the only real variable in the experiment is whether one commits to the actual attempt to recreate – in the imagination – the act of walking back and forth from one chair to the next. The only possible failure is a failure to imagine. Such an exercise ignores the supposed boundary between thought and materiality and instead begins the process of training the imagination into purposeful material form. Non-choreography.

Non-choreography? Isn't that what happens when scripts go off-script and apply themselves to life in counter-intuitive ways? When a chair gets in my head, not in some safe creative way but in that most disorienting of vertiginous and psychic ways that results in a different kind of relationship to the world? A readjustment to the posture of the imagination. Wearing a chair inside my head. The endgame of *On the Ceiling* is no mere critique of technological constraints but a speculative proposition made possible by thinking in off-label ways.

## Going Off-Script

The idea of scripting the off-script is abstract, but the stakes of such a project are quite literal, collapsing the space between theory and practice in favour of embodied experimentation and exploration. The off-script leverages media against materiality for transformative effect – creating what the artist micha cárdenas calls a form of "transreal aesthetics."[5] For cárdenas, the transreal portends to an explicitly technological situation in which boundaries between the real and the virtual have been fragmented beyond clear recognition. Importantly, instead of trying to reconcile this fragmentation, cárdenas seeks to exploit it as a way to use reality itself as an artistic medium.[6] This strikes me as a most elegant extension of François Laruelle's concept of non-philosophy, which predicts in some ways the object-oriented claim of aesthetics as "first-philosophy" by proposing performative proximity as the final solution of philosophical engagement.[7] That is, for Laruelle, philosophy aspires to be photographic, scientific, technological in its thinking, but in so doing reveals the explicit demand to live out – philosophically – a kind of thinking that is "instigated by the artificial stimulation of perception."[8] Photography is the ambassador of virtuality.

## The Provocation

What would happen if we thought of micha cárdenas as the virtual realization of François Laruelle's concept of the non-philosophical, pushing philosophy into the embodied space of the transreal? And what would happen if we then tried to think of photography (and non-photography) from this perspective – as a transreal practice unsatisfied with its usual documentary role and instead insisting on an ability to rescript the very realities it pretends to passively and neutrally represent – with all the real and material consequences, and deep philosophical implications such a position would imply?

## The Short Form

**micha cárdenas** is a trans-Latinx artist and theorist and the star of this juxtaposition, a creative thinker that inspires me with her theory of the "transreal" and her insistence on reality itself as an artistic medium. It's an idea that can be so compelling because it holds in tension the promise of virtuality and the very real positionalities of flesh and bodies, insisting on artistic positionality as a way to call the question on identity and power. cárdenas has enacted these ideas in projects ranging from immersive performances in virtual environments to real-time dance performances and other artistic and political interventions. What the projects all have in common is an embracing of the transreal, which eschews argumentative method, opting instead to "create resonances" within the multiple worlds made possible by new technologies.[9] An imagination focused, then, on possibility rather than proof, beyond truth but accountable – in activist ways – to lived circumstances.

**François Laquelle** is a French philosopher who first charmed me with his idea that philosophy is born as a "photographic catastrophe," that is, as a failed attempt to articulate observation and not as a reflective rendering of perspectives on the real.[10] Laruelle, in fact, is quite clear that he does not see photography as perception at all, but as simulation – and not of the world itself, but of "science." He calls it non-philosophy and refuses to define it – instead suggesting that the question of definition must be replaced by a question of speculative (aesthetic) usability.[11] This is not, however, operationalized philosophy; it is user experience design, a purely technological thinking of the science of the imagination for the ways it collapses into performance. Laruelle refuses opposition, insisting – in similar ways to thinkers such as Karen Barad and others – on the quantum notion of superposition as an alternative to the competitive logic of usual philosophical analysis.[12]

What I'm proposing, then, is to consider cárdenas as a creative sequel to Laruelle – an artist who moves through non-philosophy to the other side where virtuality is no longer simply a metaphor and the real strength of the "non" is not its ability to resolve the paradoxes of philosophical method but to enable the scientific treatment of the imaginary itself. The transreal is quantum pataphysics (or pataphysics with a conscience).

## Workshop for Potential Reality

Reality is overrated, especially when seen as a scientific or philosophical construct – as if any human formulation of reality could really be held accountable to the diversity of worlds we collectively inhabit (without even yet factoring in inhuman worlds and non-human worlds, thought worlds, pretend worlds, panic worlds, algorithmic worlds). Reality is a rogue concept, unaccountable to interpretation, despite (or perhaps exactly to spite) the virtuosic ambitions of any "theory of everything." To paraphrase Jean Baudrillard, if reality actually existed, it would not care one bit what we thought about it.[13] But what about those more contemporary theories of reality that embrace paradox and uncertainty, thought perhaps most romantically by quantum propositions of warped passages, entanglements, and superposition? In some of these formulations, Baudrillard's logic fails, expectation does impact outcome, as if reality were a lot more vulnerable than we had thought. Baudrillard argued that reality dies at the hand of excess – multiple realities make impossible the authority of any given one, dispersed into the beautiful postmodern ambiguity of "possibility."[14] But what if he was wrong? What if the multiple was not an argument against the singular, but just a different way of looking? What if analytic assessment is simply the wrong way to look at it? What if, instead of philosophy, what is really needed is just the opposite?

This, as I take it (or as I simplify it, distil it – faithfully or not) is the project behind François Laruelle's concept of non-philosophy. I started reading Laruelle because he offered me a new perspective on photography – the idea that the camera performs what philosophy never can, a naive technical capture that doesn't realize the power of its own action.[15] Refusing the idea of photography as a reflection of the world, Laruelle instead speaks of photographic capture as a "flash" of light, an imposed illumination that artificially stages a moment – that, in fact, creates the very concept of the moment in this process.[16] The moment, then, is a technical intervention, a "double of the world" but not in a metaphoric way; rather as a catastrophe – a quantum "superposition" of philosophy itself.[17] What photography thus creates is an additional and parallel mode of understanding that sits in a privileged social and philosophical position because its technical identity is indifferent to affected complaint. I learned quickly, however, that Laruelle is a thinker who understands too well that the task of philosophy is not to capture the world but to engage it, or – in his words – to ask how it can be put to use.[18] And so too for the camera; for Laruelle, performance is key, exceptions are to be coveted, and the endgame of philosophy (and photography) is immersion in a sustainable fiction of its own making. He calls it non-philosophy. I read it as a science of imaginary solutions.

To link Laruelle's thought to pataphysics – Alfred Jarry's "science of imaginary solutions" – may not seem intuitive, but for me the linkages are clear.[19] Laruelle anchors his speculations in science (as opposed – I assume – to poetry), seeking performative solutions with use-value rather than idle solutions with only theoretical applicability. He gravitates towards imaginary numbers, especially the square root of −1, a key anchor point for Jarry as well.[20] His propositions seek tangibility. Laruelle's non-philosophy, seen in this way, is not a mode of thought but a tactic for constructing relationships with the world, creating "[a] moment when thought in its turn becomes a form of art."[21] Nowhere is this more clear to me than in Laruelle's notion of "x-fiction," a generic extension of his concepts of non-philosophy, non-photography, and others, into the realm of non-x – a conceptual affiliation that for me finds beautiful resonance with the Collège de Pataphysique and their equivalent concept of ou-x-po: "Ou-X-Po [is] a generalization of the concept of the Oulipo … 'Ou' signifies 'to open'(ouvroir). 'Po' is for 'potential,' (potentiel), 'X,' in each distinct case, signifies the domain of activity designated by the first syllable of the word."[22]

Laruelle's pataphysics, if one were to be constituted, would revolve around the mechanism by which performance guarantees proximity to an imaginary solution (or x-fiction) – what John Ó Maoilearca calls Laruelle's "posture" but is not as simple as a bodily position.[23] Instead, read posture in that sense of Chevillard's chair, a prosthesis put on in order to deliver tangible effects on one's world. In his own words, Laruelle's x-fiction is "not an artificial perception of the World (this would suppose the philosophical model of perception) but an artificial science or a technological simulation of science."[24] The endgame of x-fiction – seen as a science of performance rather than a game of philosophy – is a workshop for potential reality, a reworking of the virtual interface by which the real manifests in its philosophical performance.

## Reality Flexing

Forget the real; or rather make it a generic variable devoted to philosophical action rather than a platform for ontological virtuosity. In fact, forget the virtuosic too, except insofar as it overextends itself into material consequence. That's the lesson of Laruelle's x-fiction, but it's also the shortcoming of Laruelle's work, which – despite its emphasis on usability and engagement – remains in uncomfortable tension with its own reflection: caught in the caveat that thinking and philosophy be thought and philosophized as their own forms of performance. I actually agree with this sentiment and appreciate the space this makes for thought as a form of artistic engagement – though even a cursory look at the history of twentieth- and twenty-first-century (Western) art will reveal a robust collection of artists who have found ways to do exactly this. To Laruelle's credit, he acknowledges art as a non-philosophical activity – yet I struggle to read his own texts as performances. In the same way as Jean Baudrillard's photography failed to capture the absences he himself found so compelling, Laruelle's texts – while inspiring and thought-provoking as philosophical objects – fail (for me, at least) as performances. They are not, in themselves, non-philosophical (though I imagine many *arguments* could be made to the contrary – a beautiful irony).

Remember that this proposition unfolds in a post-reality context in which arguments hold no sway, and in which practice is key: non-philosophy "exhausts itself as an immanent practice rather than as a program."[25] This is where the work of the artist is key, since – as micha cárdenas eloquently puts it, the work of the artist is to "create believability," especially when dealing with non-artistic or real-world contexts.[26] And indeed such is the project of cárdenas herself, articulating her process as one designed to "create resonances" rather than proving an argument.[27] She calls it "transaesthetics," and I think of it as a perfect artistic response to the concept of non-philosophy – going beyond the artistic to "use reality [itself] as a medium."[28] In cárdenas's words, "Building on the notion of 'trans' from 'transgender,' I propose that transferal aesthetics cross the boundaries of realities created by a fragmentation of reality that occurred as a result of postmodern theory and emerging technologies."[29] In her own work as an artist, cárdenas most famously spent a straight 365 hours immersed in the 3D virtual environment of Second Life as a metaphor for the year-long requirement of "real life experience" that transgender people are required to fulfil in order to receive gender confirmation surgery.[30] The project was called *Becoming*

*Dragon*, and her avatar, notably, was non-human – a dragon named Axdel Slade, onto which the artist's sight and body movements were mapped, mimicking her real-time actions in her studio with avatar movements in Second Life.[31] Created in 2008, this piece continues to hold its own, more than ten years later, as a testament to the destiny of the virtual – not simply a transaesthetic remapping of an individual body, but a virtual (technological) promise of potentiality. Recoding the real.

While cárdenas's work goes well beyond the question of photography, engaged as she is in the political and activist search for social justice and new relationships with virtual technologies, I believe it is also relevant in a relatively literal way to the question of the image. Inherent in cárdenas's performance is a promise that I believe is made by all photography – a promise of superposition – it just goes unnoticed until that moment when I seek to remap my relationship with technology. Virtuality offers this kind of remapping too – perhaps more easily because it does not require a relinquishing of one reality in favour of the other. It superimposes – head-mounted immersion as the superimposed sight of real and technological eyes; body-mapped motion as the superimposition of real and virtual performance. It is a doubling – a metaphor made real in the sense that cárdenas's body is both human and dragon; species and cross-species; asking after the parameters of assigned performance categories and their possibilities for re-assignment.

Laruelle calls it an identity that is "performed without an act of performance," "a program-without-programming or at the very least a program for de-programming."[32] cárdenas simply calls it "reality_flexing,"[33] a concept I think becomes proportionally more radical as it becomes – as it is for cárdenas – integrated beyond the act of performance as an ambition for a new form of life, simply called "living."

## Pataphysics with a Conscience

For the sake of argument, let's collapse the idea that metaphor is metaphoric and consider the possibility that poets and artists have long understood the concept of superposition in ways that have deep social potential. Let's also collapse the implied rhetorical distance between language and its manifestation – refusing the concept of metaphor its literary privilege as a safe, aesthetic way to double the world. Let's instead just live in a doubled world, thinking through the ways that doubled thinking (the literally metaphoric) can actually serve to doubly matter rather than construct zones of aesthetic consideration that sit at a safe contemplative distance from those things we call real, whatever that might be. I guess that's social superposition. Literally metaphoric living. Like bringing art and life together in ways that don't respect a need to differentiate but that hopefully still sustain an aspiration towards making difference meaningful. Perhaps what matters is not the reality of the ideas but the gravity of the situation, thinking explicitly of gravity as a force acting on the world – and thinking of creative intervention as an equivalent companion force.

cárdenas's work has this kind of gravity for me, breaking from a linear ontology of the real, refusing not just the category but the categorical limits ontology puts onto imaginations and social engagement. Her ideas have materiality imagined into them – sometimes virtual materialities like her work in Second Life; other times materiality in the more tactile sense, artistic objects designed to help imagine tangible social transformation. She has made networked hoodies designed to help people feel safe;[34] she has proposed DIY bulletproof clothing (built from compositing layers of recycled rubber from tires);[35] she invites viewers in augmented reality environments for a virtual contemplation of life in an age of ecological disaster.[36] And yet, in each case the proposals are not merely utilitarian or innovation-driven (though innovation is, of course, part of the language of new media and technology-based artistic work). Instead, I think it's worth noting and emphasizing that there is an artistic aspiration inherent in each of her projects – a sense that we are not there (at the aspirational social destination) yet, that the propositions are thus still speculative, perhaps possible but only by embracing the chance of collectively rewriting the scripts of the real itself. The transformative power of cárdenas's thought lies in its refusal of the boundary between the poetic and the real – literally. This is no metaphor, or if it is, it is one that redefines the metaphoric without the aesthetic distance usually associated with artistic concepts; this is a superposition of art and reality.

But think about that in the context of photography, where every picture is a duplicate that both is and is not its double – representing (perhaps) but also re-casting in ways that disrupt representational ideology by superimposing another (more dramatic) version of the real on top of that moment that would otherwise be lost or gone. Literal metaphors, photography is the simplest iteration of virtualization, at its core a system of replication that takes the world as its source material. Like all technology. The trick is to find ways to make such systems fail – to pack a photograph with layers of tire rubber (here I'm being metaphoric of course) such that it too finds a bulletproof possibility. One could call it photographing vampires – or perhaps better, pataphysics with a conscience.

There is an unspoken rule that pataphysicians should refrain from calling their work pataphysics. It is as if to name an imaginary engagement for what it is risks compromising the social and political power of its gesture. Certainly this is also often true of philosophy and indeed of art, reduced to material objects for contemplation and subject to commentary or elitist speculation rather than allowed its place in that social order which might be still called real (whatever that might be). Immersed in the virtuality of "reason." cárdenas asks:

> If reason itself is a western invention, part of colonialism, then is the future of thought to be poetry? Poetry of the flesh, intensive gradations of feeling and wordless thought, movements inside the body, states where planes of color bleed and shift into each other?[37]

It is hard to resist a cheer at the idea of future thought adopting a predominantly poetic form – but truth be told poetry alone can probably not get rid of reason. By contrast, then, to follow both Laruelle and cárdenas into the territory of the virtual is not only to refuse the linear language of technical thought but also to insist on superimposing it always with its double – the poetic and metaphoric and performative and self-reflexive and any other mode of thought that can cultivate the kind of gravity needed to contribute to the project of obliterating reality as it is in favour of creating different forms of futurity. Superposition and metaphor as tools for duplicating the real differently such as to insist on always holding together multiple possibilities for tomorrow.

## Non-Choreography

Forget photography, says the photographer (in a book about photography!). "The essence of photography is not itself 'photographic,'" says Laruelle,[38] echoing Heidegger's equivalent claim for the broader category of technology.[39] Every photograph is a moment made to be forgotten but still carrying forward the power of implanted imagination – part trust object, part reality flex.

The essence of photography is thus doubled: performative and prohibitive. Prohibitive because photography carries with it the technological scripts of documentary truth that argue that self-evidence is self-evident – a prophetic conceit that forms the usual stage of image encounter. But photography has a double side too – the performance that catalyses the documentary moment, and this is where the possibility for engagement resides. Remember the metaphor – the scripted documentary moment is not untrue; it is a superposition of time and intentionality on a world that would otherwise have simply continued on script. Except that this time it's not a Photoshop tutorial; it is a project for workshopping proximities to reality. It is an experiment in reality_flexing and non-choreography in which terms of engagement are repossessed, twisted, and performed differently, played with in ways that don't have to make sense because they are not trying to map new truths but to simply explore, experience, exist. It's not really ironic that the potential of the camera as a reality-bending tool hasn't yet been fully embraced; it's tragic. Get over truth – the camera is over it already. The essence of photography is metaphoric.

Thinking back, then, to the exercise that catalysed this discussion, I propose that *On the Ceiling*, as a participatory project, has the potential to ease the entry into the transreal, thinking about posture as attitude, thinking about interface as possibility, thinking about a chair – a chair, what more familiar and non-threatening object is possible? – as a device that has already fully colonized the imagination of the person who uses it. It is an exercise in non-choreography. Non-choreography emerges to challenge the behavioural scripts that mark technological engagement by insisting on a creative proximity to the performance of virtual interaction. Against the scripting of technological behaviours, an absurdist choreography of engagement. **Non-choreography** is an attempt to reassess relationships between humans and those inanimate and generic companions that already script the virtual architecture of the human imagination.

# 5

# Digital Darkness

**Exercise 5: Shine a Laser Pointer at the Camera**

**Framing statement:** In his book *Towards a Philosophy of Photography*, the philosopher Vilém Flusser suggests that technology has a tendency to over-write human ways of understanding the world. He likens the process to magic – replacing human experience and knowledge with a technical likeness we believe even more than we believe our own thoughts, feelings, or intuitions.[1] We see this in medicine, where bodies are increasingly understood through testing and genetic codes; we see this in social living, where identities are increasingly represented by data profiles; we see this in knowledge, where databases replace libraries and information circulates at the speed of access. Under the regime of this sort of technical imagination, we risk becoming simply another source of information for algorithmic systems of computational learning and knowledge.

For Flusser, the only appropriate response to this technological context is to attempt to speak back to the systems that code our ways of knowing and behaving, a game of tag in which we are only human to the extent that we can understand how to remix, respond, or re-imagine the ways in which technology creates and represents the worlds we inhabit.[2] It is less a revolution than an attempt to insist on a relationship with the technologies that monitor us as we move through life.

**Guidelines:** This project asks you to speak back to the camera. In order to participate, take a photograph of somebody shining a laser pointer at the camera. When aimed just right, this will cause a lens flare that can be treated as an artistic element. Consider staging your intervention in a public location. Consider using a publicly available surveillance camera, web camera, or traffic camera as your target. You should be able to see what they see on any mobile device, thus confirming that your intervention has been seen.

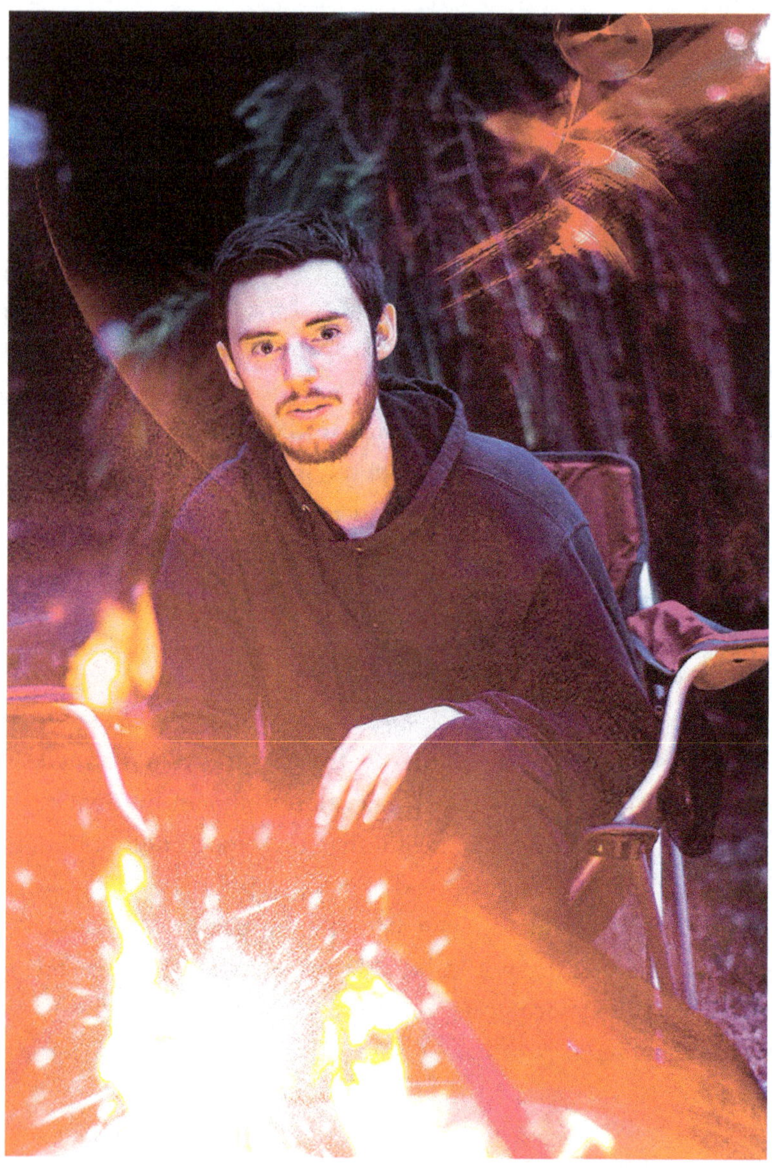

Figure 5.  Heather McAllister, *Laser Pointer Tag*, photograph, 2019

## Laser Pointer Tag

A man sits in a camping chair. He wears a hoodie and an ambiguous expression. He is looking at me – that is, he is looking at the camera, but also looking at me. He makes clear that he knows he is in a photograph and that I should know that he knows. Around him, strange abstract lights dance without moving, red arcs across the image scene, technological artefacts and conjured manifestations, or perhaps simply optical defects exploited for their flare. This is a HOLGA moment for the twenty-first century, an expansion of the always trendy counter-photographic craze where low-budget cameras are used for their defects, emphasizing the ways that poorly built cameras can add personality to a picture through light leaks and filters. Except that in this image it is not the camera but the lens that is exploited – the usually invisible aperture of the device used to undermine the transparency of the apparatus.

A laser pointer is the culprit, held low in the screen and targeting the camera that itself uses the same infrared beam for its automatic focus. A re-targeting is in play, and a game of tag is initiated by the attempt to disrupt the dynamics of optical precision by emphasizing the vulnerability of the very lens used to instrumentalize visual capture. It's illegal to shine a laser pointer at planes for this very reason – the refractions caused by focused and targeted light can blind those looking out from within the optical sensors. The irony of course is that the very technical mechanism used for precision autofocus – a narrow spectrum infrared beam of light – is criminalized in the hands of those it usually targets.

Not so here. Beaming back, this man's campfire is an electronic optical flare. His focus is on his own precision vision, targeting the apparatus that captures his image. The result is part disruption part choreographed interaction, a dance in which the camera itself is no longer simply the dominant lead but a co-partner in the project of image creation. Forced away from its own autofocus, the camera is subjected to a refocusing gaze, a gesture of reciprocity, a flare.

A camera has no flare – its infrared beam is meant to exactly not be seen. But that doesn't mean one cannot adopt a positional flare when being photographed, add character to the technical image by precisely causing a rupture of optical virtuosity by exploiting the vulnerability of the mechanism. Precision-crafted glass is both the corneal lens of the technical predator and the mechanism for diffraction that allows for reciprocal response. In a strange way, it's both transactional and relational – two different modes of looking that I never really thought I'd find happening at the same time. It's algorithmic and empathetic. Well, sort of. I don't really think the camera cares, except that it still reacts, which might then be thought of as a form of optical caring. A technical and non-human recognition of being seen.

## Fashioned with Flare

Several years ago there was a brilliant design project that rose to popular acclaim by using make-up to frustrate optical face recognition technology. It was called CV Dazzle, and its aim was exactly that: to dazzle the camera or make it look sideways in some way that could evade the technical ideology of optical capture. Instead of facial recognition, something else: an "anti-face" or a dazzle. From the project website:

> CV Dazzle explores how fashion can be used as camouflage from face-detection technology, the first step in automated face recognition. It is a concept and strategy, not a pattern or product, and it is always designed relative to a specific algorithm and unique to each face … The name CV Dazzle was inspired by a type of World War I naval camouflage called Dazzle, which used cubist-inspired designs to break apart the visual continuity of a battleship and conceal its orientation and size. Likewise, CV Dazzle uses avant-garde hairstyling and makeup designs to break apart the continuity of a face. Since facial-recognition algorithms rely on the identification and spatial relationship of key facial features, like symmetry and tonal contours, one can block detection by creating an "anti-face."[3]

But my point in evoking this project is not simply to praise the intervention that aesthetic reconfiguration might accomplish but to appreciate the way the project also acknowledges the incommensurability of aesthetics as an essential component of optical resistance. No templates, for the simple reason that the algorithms CV Dazzle targets are not static apparatuses of capture but neural networks capable of active learning and growth. Their morphemes are images: "face detection datasets and neural networks have learned how to detect faces with makeup or facial accessories. It is also not recommended that you post your looks on Instagram or Facebook, as those too will be used to make neural networks stronger."[4]

Who dazzles who? The black box of machine learning meets the creative accoutrements of aesthetic resistance in a dance best destined to happen in the dark. That is, each system – the technical systems of intelligent recognition and the aesthetic systems of optical disruption – understands the other as an evolving agent in an ongoing conversation. Each seeks to see and yet to not be seen in return, and yet each also has a particular flare and dazzle to its operational ideology. The dialogic potential of the interaction relies on remaining unresolved – ambiguity is not simply a side effect but the main point. For a system designed to resolve faces, this, then, is an opening up to a different kind of communication, shrouded in digital darkness.

Digital darkness? Isn't that what happens when, relieved from the imperative of definitive resolution, the AI system encounters something new? It might manifest simply as a series of trouble-shooting sub-routines, but in the metaphor I am trying to build, there is something more that occurs. Maybe the possibility of a relationship, marked by the increased time spent in optical interaction. Maybe even something more – an augmentation of the experiential moment. **Laser Pointer Tag** is an exercise in digital darkness – no documentation; only performance. It's all about the dazzle and flare.

## Placebo Ergo Sum

In an age of pervasive technical domination, the power to build relationships relies on an aesthetic catalyst, something to slow down the dazzle and flare of the camera and provide more ambiguous spaces of representation. This is a version of what philosopher Vilém Flusser calls (purposeful) disobedience, noting that the magic of representation – as a technical system – is that it binds us to its logic, even when we understand its trick, despite understanding itself. Thought, for Flusser, is inadequate as a means of resistance since thinking is itself the actual material medium used by the camera.[5] The trick, then, is not to think about images differently, but to think differently about technical thought itself – one version of which might be to implement what artist and theorist Katherine Behar calls "decelerationist aesthetics" as a way to survive the ubiquitous systems of technical capture by finding ways to create pockets of slowness in an ever accelerating world.[6] It could also be seen as a form of counter-magic – thinking about technical ideology not as an information system but as a context for engagement.

## The Provocation

What would happen if we thought of Katherine Behar as the second act in the story of magic told by Vilém Flusser, no longer held under the rapture of the photograph but looking for ways to exploit sorcery in the name of building relationships with systems of technical power. That is, while Flusser prescribes disobedience as a form of freedom from the apparatus, it is Behar who puts this idea into action – not only for images but for any technical system that perpetuates indoctrination and expectation.

## The Short Form

**Katherine Behar** is an artist and theorist and the star of this juxtaposition, a thinker that inspires me to remember the ways technology operates on social and emotional registers – and whose work I take as a beacon for thinking the relationship between digital culture and art. Principal to my admiration are Behar's concepts of "decelerationist aesthetics"[7] and "Botox ethics"[8] that can be such powerful ways of rethinking the world because they work in entirely counter-intuitive ways. Forget the efficiency metrics of technical speed and instead indulge in forms of counter-magic. Forget the imperative to appear and instead find ways to play with the ambiguities of darkness, numbness, ambiguity. Forget intelligence and instead work towards forms of what Behar calls "artificial ignorance."[9]

**Vilém Flusser** is a Brazilian and Czechoslovakian-born philosopher that has been central to my rethinking of the medium of photography, principally for the way he situates the camera as an apparatus that is both technical and magical at the same time.[10] This seemingly counter-intuitive claim situates Flusser, for me, as an observer of the cosmological tendencies of technological culture. In this, I take Flusser as a meta-thinker of technology, attuned specifically to the production of ideology that comes as an effect of living with the camera. While the camera itself may be premised on a harnessing of light, Flusser gravitates to the concept of the "black box" in order to discuss the hidden operations of technical systems – thus making darkness, not light, the guiding epistemology of technical systems of thought.[11]

What I am proposing, then, is to consider the ways in which Behar's work provides a performative frame of reference for how to engage with Flusser's conceptualization of the "black box" as a system of manufactured darkness. Against the dominant context of shadows as emblems of technical magic, a self-possessed drive towards the dark, the slow, the ignorant, the glitchy as the default stage upon which the performance of life continues. Not the attempt to dispel the sway of technology but to find counter-magic in the form of cheats and hacks and unaccounted ambiguities that can be mobilized as ways to create new or different forms of space. No documentation, only performance. If cameras set in motion ways of thinking that bind me to representation – thinking me into (representational) being – then the trick is perhaps to refuse representation in favour of a certain kind of alternative story-telling. *Placebo ergo sum*: I hallucinate myself into (non-representational) existence.[12]

## Manufactured Darkness

The future of photography will be found in the dark – but not the kind of darkness that results from simply turning out the lights. Photographic darkness is more like the silence produced by white noise: a darkness produced by overexposure, an overshadowing whose result is to port material vision into a hallucination produced by technical systems. This kind of darkness is the kind that is impossible not to see – it is a ubiquitous darkness that circulates under the sign of technical impartiality. The camera is the original black box, after all, and thus a forebear of the complex technical and intelligent systems of today. As Vilém Flusser so aptly puts it: "All apparatuses (not just computers) are calculating machines and in this sense 'artificial intelligences', the camera included."[13] And for me, Flusser can be such a perfect foil for this line of thought because I take him to believe first and foremost that the primary objective of cameras – and thus of all technical systems – is not simply the production of images but the actual production of ideology: "Their intention is not to change the world but to change the meaning of the world."[14] Flusser also states, "The hypothesis proposed here thus argues that we think like this because we think in photographic categories: because the photographic universe has programmed us to think in a post-historical way."[15] I have always loved Flusser's work for its particularly technical way of critiquing the technical – from cameras to evolution to magic and ideology – and for me, in the question of the camera can be found a beautiful condensation of his thought in ways that counter-intuitively aggregate the technical and the magical. This because, for Flusser, the space of the image is none other than "the world of magic" – premised first and foremost on the increasingly pervasive fact that while we have bound ourselves irrevocably to a reliance on the complex technical operations of informatic systems, we are increasingly incapable of reverse engineering the solutions given to us by technical systems.[16]

This might seem like a pedantic point, but its consequence is significant – a disaggregation of the historical categories of information and knowledge. If "enlightenment" thinking used the conflation of these two terms to claim an illuminated perspective as metaphor for wisdom, quite the opposite would now be more appropriate – a darkening in which knowledge comes to us as solutions produced by technical systems that no longer show their work. The black box is the authority – the mystery of the black box is that its process is truly opaque, invisible to the human gaze because its logic no longer belongs to that of human capacity.[17]

Flusser has a term for a device that produces knowledge of this kind – a "preparatus" – describing the function of the photographic apparatus as a production of ideology (preparing me, so to speak) that can be so persuasive because it masquerades as a device that seems to tell me things I already know (re-presenting the world as already familiar).[18] But technical systems perform logic without themselves being accountable to logic – at least not to logic of a human form. In this way, the image – disaggregated from the procedural link between the (human) world and its representation – functions more as a catalyst than an anchor point, producing technical artefacts that circulate with the power of suspended disbelief. Photographs, for Flusser, are thus indicative of a more general cultural slippage that conflates optical representation with the technical magic of intelligent systems. Technically generated hallucinations become the new form of representation.[19]

Thus the power of the camera (and of all technical systems) is not simply the production of hallucination but the production of a social imagination in which hallucination circulates with the materiality of authentic experience. And his question is how to oppose a "preparatus" given that the entire operation of such technical systems is anchored in a pedagogical thrust that becomes a demand for trust, justified by the authority of information itself.

To follow Flusser in the attempt to think against this kind of technical programming is to aspire towards a decolonization of the image, moving loyalties away from the technical systems that generate (dominant) truth and instead attuning to the darkness that emerges as a marker of lived precarity that can never live up to – or keep up with – the representational speed of the image. Against the logic of representation as a horizon of veracity, Flusser – for me – is a harbinger of a new kind of social imagination, one that lives in the darkness produced by black-boxed systems of technical thought that now set the dominant representational pillars of human knowledge. Technical solutions are no longer the point. When living in the dark, what matters is the incommensurability of the experienced moment; images hereafter will only service the production of experience.

## Emotional Contagion

In the early 2000s Facebook conducted a secret study of the influencing power of images, pumping images deemed happy to a certain sub-set of its users and unhappy images to another. The goal was to assess the possibility of what was called, in the study, "emotional contagion."[20] What they found was unsurprising – that exposure to a particular inflection of imagery had a direct correlation to the mood of the subsequent posts by users. The artificially augmented emotional ecosystem catalysed hallucinatory response in exactly the way Flusser might have theorized. But while Flusser's thought lets me understand some of the nuances of why a strategy of this sort would work, it does not change the fact that it does work; despite my understanding of the technical magic in play, my moods respond as moods do to the digital ecosystem of artificial affect.

This incommensurability of affective experience – the way that emotional influence trumps intellectual understanding – has, for me, been most inspirationally engaged by Katherine Behar's description of this Facebook study as an emblematic instance of the twenty-first technical century tendency to align ourselves emotionally with the technical representations that form the backbone of digital and networked culture.[21] Behar's theorization leads her less to a redemption of the emotional subject and more towards an insistence that it has become increasingly urgent to understand ourselves as living within an ecosystem already reading mood as a variable that is subject to (neoliberal) influence. What is an influencer after all, if not a conducer of affect – an agent of emotional contagion, for good or for bad is perhaps beside the point. It's a well-worn line of thought in the history of technological thinking that the endgame of technology is to act as an agent of ideological refashioning. What's different here is that Behar understands the lived implications of such a perspective – situating the power of mood as operating in excess of understanding, indeed framing experience (with all its inflections of mood) as the primary site of contestation in a technically mediated environment.

It's important to this line of thinking to also note that Behar is not governed by a romantic notion of enabled selves or enlightenment logic that conventionally binds informatic accomplishment to human progress. Instead, for Behar, the subject is suspect, especially in its Western neoliberal form where the individualized subject is already pre-formulated to exclude non-normative positionalities, especially those of women, people of colour, and those managing disability. Subjecthood in this form is "the damaging legacy of humanist exceptionalism."[22] Behar writes: "Primarily a white, male, heterosexual, abled, rational heir to Enlightenment humanism, the subject is a red herring … [the subject] is something to be questioned, not prized."[23] Instead of holding the potential for enlightened self-reflection, the technological reinforcement of subject-positionality is simply another tactic of control: "emotional contagion." As Behar puts it (in a slightly different context): "My data sold back to me, thereby transforming me bit by bit into the subject it already knew me to be. Producing 'me.'"[24]

Behar's reconceptualization of this landscape is provocative – a purposeful attempt to work against the idea that technology links to a representation of lived experience. For Behar, "The trend toward privileging connectivity results in a fetishization of liveliness."[25] She calls this "vivophilia," critiquing the ways that representations of liveliness construct a context of expectation and social norms that require a certain performance of experience for the sake of the image.[26] And, instead of embracing the living representations that circulate as alibis for experience, Behar proposes the counter-intuitive but thought-provoking possibility of "embracing necrophilia" as a philosophical refusal of the living images of technology. Imagine the attempt to hear silence when a white noise machine is at full volume, and then extract from that the analogy to a digital circulation of "vivophilic" images. How might I make space to apprehend the incommensurability of experience in a world full of images that tell me who I am? How can I see darkness in a world filled with blinding light?

Behar's proposition is to adopt what she calls "Botox ethics," using the metaphor of Botox injection as a way to refuse the expected performances of vivophilic living.[27] Numbing the muscles of the face such that one appears without expression, numbing one's own expectations such as to realize that the camera does not see experience and thus simulates it instead. The point is not to refuse appearances but to refuse to play along to the scripts of emotional influence that images generate. In Behar's words, Botox "wants to be left alone."[28] That one may not recognize one's emotional presence in an image is not an argument against the strategy – rather, it is a concession that any recognition was itself already more of a technical production than a marker of individual presence. Botox ethics aligns itself with that which remains unrepresented as a political and ideological strategy, insisting on a form of emotional presence that short circuits the usual play of technical relationality, re-inflecting the relationship in ways that make it more ambiguous, producing counter-moods to the emotional contagion at the core of vivophilic representation: "Its self-fashioning is the corporeal practice of inhibiting life within oneself. It is a praxis of practicing death."[29]

Such a re-orientation is precisely non-photographic in practice, and as such also perfectly photographic in spirit. A screen-saver face. "Existing as a way of insisting."[30] It is a theory of "inhospitality" towards the technical image.[31]

## Deceleration

Two Amazon Alexas sit across from each other at a table, one attempting to guess a number known only to the other. Alexa guesses. Alexa evaluates the answer. The process continues until the correct number is chosen. It's both a cynical game and an illustrious art project by Katherine Behar:

> In *Knock Knock*, two speech-enabled smart devices go head-to-head when one Alexa tries to guess a cryptographic key known only to the other. Their guessing game begins like the familiar children's game prompt, *"I'm thinking of a number ..."* However, this number relies on SHA-256, the same encryption used by blockchain technology. The only way to win is through "brute force," that is, by trying random 64-digit combinations until luck prevails.[32]

At first glance it would seem that the point of the piece is the irony created by having two Alexas engage in an algorithmic guessing game, putting high tech to use for human entertainment. The technical joke is a joke on us, however, since the encryption algorithms guarantee that no real information will be exchanged, even in the event of a correctly guessed number. Run through SHA256 technology,

Alexa is not trying to actually guess a number but a verification code.[33] Thus the real point of the piece has nothing to do with information at all – not really – and everything to do with the time and space held by the process as it unfolds.

The absurdity of course is that this duration depends on the failure of one Alexa to guess the verification key generated by the other – but in some ways the longer it takes the better – the correct guess would only end the game, fulfilling the promise of what we already knew would happen eventually. The longer it lasts, the more I find myself in relation to the piece: "Connectivity is not the same as (and maybe is opposite to) relationality."[34] In a kind of reverse magic, *Knock Knock* dilates technical time, elongating the duration of the game by requiring that each guess be spoken in human time, in words, manifest with an audible presence in the room. Behar calls this a "decelerationist aesthetics"[35] and contrasts it against modes of thought that argue for augmented and accelerated thought as the only ways to keep pace with technological advance. Remember slow food? Remember slow scholarship? In a beautiful way, *Knock Knock* uses technical virtuosity as an alibi for slowness – what presents itself as an evidencing of an encryption failsafe in fact has the effect of reversing the temporal virtuosity of the systems themselves. One might call it a form of long exposure cryptography:

In decelerationist aesthetics, the aesthetic properties, proclivities, and performances of objects come to defy the accelerationist imperative to be nimbly individuated. Decelerationist aesthetics rejects atomistic, liberal, humanist subjects; this unit of self is too consonant with capitalist relations and functions. Instead, decelerationist aesthetics favors transhuman sociality embodied in particulate, mattered objects; the aesthetic form of such objects resists capitalist speed and immediacy by taking back and taking up space and time.[36]

But think about that in the context of photography. What happens when a responsive system is put into a feedback loop? Isn't that what's so great about photography, and so humbling? That it creates exactly this same sort of feedback loop for the human psyche? Two versions of me put into the same space – one looking at the other, the first a perceptive agent, the second a non-perceptive artefact of presence. The game is to guess which one is more real, which is an unanswerable question since it depends entirely on the context in which the question is asked. For my great-grandchildren (if the world lasts that long) the image will be the only material record; for my day-to-day interactions, perhaps it's not quite the same. And it strikes me that this is an essential moment to insist on the linkage between Alexa and the camera – two devices cut from the same technical ideology of virtuosic capture.

The idea that an image could thus serve to slow down the pace of living is – at least for me – counter-intuitive, and all the more noteworthy because of it. Not a fast-capture of a moment to legitimize a moment but precisely a slowing down to the speed of forever. The photograph does not capture an instant; it creates and reinforces the ideological perspective from which instants are possible to begin with. But from the inverse perspective – seen as two Alexas talking to themselves – images have the potential to slow down experience precisely to the extent that they are seen as ecological interventions rather than agents of technical truth.

## Digital Darkness

In a digital age it is tempting to think that the darkroom has disappeared and that henceforth photography can only serve as a positivist tool for casting us into the light. But if I am to follow Behar's logic of deceleration and withholding, nothing could be further from the truth (whatever that means). Instead, images function as tools of overexposure, like white noise that cancels the sounds of the world around. Digital darkness is white noise given visual form, an over-stimulation of the visual that collapses my ability to see such that the only tools left to rely on are those of touch. But images touch me too – they are emotional agents – and thus some consideration of their impact seems necessary.

But perhaps this is not an entirely new thing to say. When I was an art student working in the (literal) dark room, it struck me that light was only one side to the photographic equation. When the lights go out (when developing film, for instance, or printing chromogenic) it is necessary to function by touch alone, feeling one's way around in the dark in order to perform the tasks of image creation. Perhaps the darkroom is simply now the more generalized state of living.

To align this with the exercise that opened this chapter, I would offer that Laser Pointer Tag, as a participatory project, is one way to turn the darkroom inside out – making it the stage of documented living. It is less a method of seeing in the dark than one of calling on the apparatus to acknowledge a state of overexposure. And so, maybe **digital darkness** isn't the context created by pervasive machine magic but just the opposite. An intentional decision to live in the dark, which means to feel one's way around even if one can still see. To live *as if* in the dark such as to remain reminded of the magic wash of intelligibility. For if intelligibility – as a marker of technical thought or algorithmic virtuosity – is truly a magic spell, then in order to break the spell I would need to relinquish a reliance on making sense. Against the high-resolution representation of truth, a purposeful alignment with the ambiguity of a world unseen. Photography is no longer a picture on a page or screen but a purposeful choice to produce darknesses and overexposures of my own.

# 6

# Conspiracy Thinking

**Exercise 6: Take a Picture of Someone Wearing a Tinfoil Hat**

**Framing statement:** In his 1927 story "The Tissue-Culture King," Julian Huxley wrote about a machine designed for mass telepathy, built as an experimental mind-control apparatus to help control a growing population.[1] To protect themselves from the radiating influence of the telepathic broadcast, the inventors of the machine wore aluminium hats, specifically designed to protect their minds from the voice of the apparatus, and by extension from the commands of algorithmic surveillance. The story has since been taken up by conspiracy theorists, psychologists, and media scholars as an example of the possibilities and dangers of living in a technologically mediated world in which the boundaries between truth, persuasion, and passionate falsities have become (perhaps purposefully) blurred.

What is perhaps the most compelling thing about a tinfoil hat, however, is not the truth or falsity of the claim that it protects the mind. Much more interesting is the possibility that by wearing such an accessory one claims one's mind as one's own. It seems a silly thing to say, but in a world filled with advertising, marketing, and propaganda, the mind may be a more contested site than we think. Literally. The idea of the tinfoil hat then stands as a metaphor for psychological precarity, acknowledging a certain vulnerability of mind that might otherwise be taken for granted. If only influence could be so easily avoided. While there is no certain way to reconcile the layers of conspiracy, spectacle, and conjecture that surround the tinfoil hat as an apparatus and a metaphor, one way to keep the inquiry alive is to simply engage with the metaphor itself.

**Guidelines:** This project seeks to animate the story of the tinfoil hat, with particular attention to the ways in which the hat becomes a metaphor for social and technological engagement. To participate, take a photograph of a person wearing a tinfoil hat. Think about the different parts of the picture – the location, the shape of the hat, the light (and other frequencies) that are touching your subject – and how those variables might represent some of the metaphoric power of the concept.

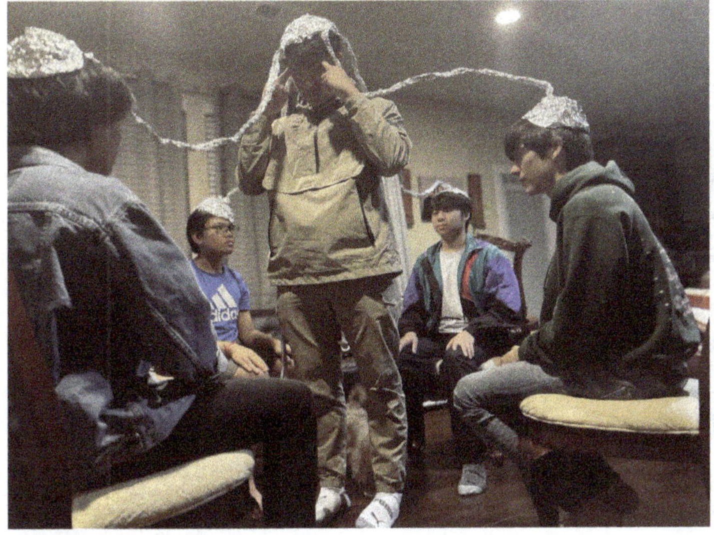

Figure 6. Brandon Kan, *Tinfoil Hats*, photograph, 2021

## Tinfoil Hats

Five men stand in a room, connected by tinfoil tubes. Well, four men stand in a room connected to a fifth man who stands in the centre, a provocative centre of attention. There are few signs to indicate whether he is speaking or listening, but one thing is sure – his demeanour shows signs of labour and intention. He is connected and so are those sat around him, and however they are connected, it is on purpose.

Something interesting happens when the connections we nurture and sustain with others are literalized, made hyper-evident as literal connections that come with material attachment and consequences. It can seem to mistake hard wires for the soft or the wet, but what if relationships and connectivity and network signals of broadcast and receive were taken literally as things in the world – as actual and tangible and material points of connection and interchange? This is an image about community and channelling and attunement and trust and power and empowerment and more.

And I stop, caught in the feeling that I am also somehow connected to the image. Are these tinfoil wires contained within the image, or are they metaphors in some way for my relationship to this situation too? I look at the picture again and I feel sucked in – like there is some kind of conceptual attraction that keeps me engaged in the possibility that I too am part of this network. Or maybe its just desire – a social network given visual form in such an eloquent way as to make me want to also sign up or sign in, to be registered, or simply to be seen.

Yet as soon as I say this to myself I am back on the outside – unseen. Private thoughts are being shared, collective worlds are being generated. And I am on the outside, watching, but not quite noticed. I know the story of tinfoil as a way to block signals, but I'm caught here by what seems to be exactly the opposite fantasy – a world in which technologies of blockage are creatively re-channelled towards the formation of relationships and community.

It might just be a performative joke – a picture staged for the camera – but I don't think so. And whether the tinfoil is just a prop or an actual technology here is maybe a nuanced and not-so-important distinction since the connectivity of the situation speaks more loudly than any particular informational content one might project onto the moment. More important than what they are saying is their capacity for speech – and more important than what they might be communicating is the fact that they seem connected, and I by contrast seem to be a disconnected but interested observer. Caught on the outside of someone else's secret.

## Attunement

In 2005 a group of graduate students at MIT – Ali Rahimi, Ben Recht, Jason Taylor, and Noah Vawter – ran a series of frequency amplification experiments on tinfoil hats, looking to see whether the rumblings of conspiracy theorists had any truth to them and if aluminium foil could really provide a shield between the mind and the world of electronic signals looking to harvest private thoughts. In theory the aluminium foil creates a rudimentary Faraday cage around the brain, capable of deflecting predatory scans and other forms of mind control, a theory that provides some explanation for how a ridiculous fashion accessory might actually serve a serious purpose. To do so they built three different varieties of aluminium hats, put them on, and proceeded to scan the hats as well as their own brains for frequency modulations as they blasted their heads with various electronic signals: sweeping ranges from AM radio to RFID, television to radar, microwaves to cellular, communication satellites to government-exclusive frequency bands, and using a high-end network analyser and a directional antenna to measure and plot the results.[2]

In an interesting plot development, the study found that wearing a tinfoil hat actually *does* serve to protect the head from a significant number of frequencies, particularly those in the range of radio waves (which is curiously the frequency band also talked about by Huxley in his story). This wasn't the only discovery they made, however – ironically, these aluminium headpieces also seemed to amplify certain *other* frequencies – those associated with exactly the bandwidths most feared by conspirators – allocated to government agencies and mobile phone corporations:

> For all helmets, we noticed a 30 db amplification at 2.6 Ghz and a 20 db amplification at 1.2 Ghz, regardless of the position of the antenna on the cranium ... Conclusion: The helmets amplify frequency bands that coincide with those allocated to the US government between 1.2 Ghz and 1.4 Ghz. According to the FCC, These bands are supposedly reserved for "radio location" (ie, GPS), and other communications with satellites. The 2.6 Ghz band coincides with mobile phone technology.[3]

Admittedly, this study reads as much as a graduate student prank as it does a serious gambit of science – the kind of wonderful play that someone with access to advanced technology might engage just because the opportunity presents itself. And while the results seem unambiguous, the question of how one engages (or dismisses) the results might vary widely. For myself, I find especially compelling the idea that the tinfoil hat may actually amplify specific frequencies of signal associated with GPS and cellular data – frequencies much more important to the twenty-first century than those radio waves that concerned Huxley and others. And I don't care if it's true or not – it's the idea of taking the experiment seriously that catches my attention most seductively, as if to turn conspiracy theory into a participatory form of active and purposeful thinking.

Conspiracy thinking? Isn't that what happens when I test an absurd hypothesis only to find that the device worn to protect myself against government mind-readers actually instead seems to make my thoughts more accessible to a technical surveillance system? And isn't it just a perfect reversal for an age in which the destiny of privacy is to be shared online in those most familiar of social media spaces where profiles are populated by vulnerability – intended perhaps for peers and loved ones but unapologetically harvested by corporate bots for the purposes of remarketing and data accumulation. Nobody really believes in privacy anymore, and certainly not when engaged in online communication. An inside-out tinfoil hat, social media simply turns up the gain on the technological broadcast of private thoughts, on our relationship to technological culture. **Tinfoil Hats** starts as a refusal but becomes a form of attunement, a broadcast amplifier for new forms of digital being.

## An Excess of Privacy

The destiny of privacy is to be shared – otherwise it would not be a thing – a truly private form of privacy would have to content itself with the incommensurable constraints of subjective living. Thus things private belong not to the order of data but to the category of secrets. Importantly, secrets need not be true or even shared to hold their power – their seductive sway has most to do with the perception of incommensurability withheld, a teasing or a challenge that operates at the level of a promise. This promise, according to Jean Baudrillard, is the operational logic of digital culture, bypassing the order of communication by engaging directly with the hyperreal – the more real than real that is bound not to informatic accountability but to the secrets I tell myself, bound to the integrity of simulation.[4] But, perhaps, secrets also operate at the level of what philosopher Johnny Golding calls "radical mattering," disregarding information as the impact factor of interpersonal exchange.[5] Beyond the reality of the situation, relationships form and experiences are shared, despite the seemingly solitary nature of a world governed by the principles of secrecy.

## The Provocation

What if Johnny Golding's theory of "radical mattering" were adopted as a horizon of accountability for the postmodern, in general, and the hyperreal, in particular – not by resolving them but by making friends with the predictive logics so seductively rendered by Jean Baudrillard? This would be to betray Baudrillard by exactly not acknowledging the distinction between the simulation and the real and instead siding in favour with the immediacy of relational engagement.

## The Short Form

**Johnny Golding** is a political philosopher who examines questions of identity, technology, and art with an eye to charting strategies for creating futures differently or otherwise. For me, Golding's conceptualization of "technologies of otherness" are paramount to my seduction with her thought – strategies for rethinking a relational approach to philosophical living, inflected by the eloquent concepts of radical mattering, and friendship.[6] Thinking through and beyond the post-structural categories of deconstruction and difference, Golding seeks ways to mark difference as a new form of philosophical accountability, making difference matter as the true horizon of living in a deconstructed world.[7] In this, and against theories of enlightened knowledge or redemptive understanding, I take Golding as a prophet of attunement, a thinker of relational politics for the ways that engagement and encounter turn into experiences that matter – a sort of philosophical UX for an age of predictive living.

**Jean Baudrillard** is French philosopher perhaps best known for his theories of simulation and the hyperreal and his argument that in digital times it no longer makes sense to think about the real.[8] Baudrillard, from my perspective, might also be the philosopher most responsible for the popularization of "post-truth" – a hallmark of postmodern thought and (for different reasons) the bane of contemporary twenty-first-century politics. But for me, the seduction of Baudrillard's thinking has nothing to do with truth; for me, the question always comes back to the stakes of the experiential moment. The seduction of the virtual only matters within a horizon where something like life is nonetheless still happening, true or post-truth, or not. In this, Baudrillard for me is the last and best of the postmodernists, insisting that the horizon of technological living is not one of logic but of seduction and calculated gambles.[9]

What I am proposing, then, is to take seriously Baudrillard's declaration of the end of the real while insisting on Golding's politics of identity and lived experience as the necessary conditions of lived encounter.[10] Privacy – overrated or not – is the key currency of digital living, not bound to data points or verified information but to the power of affective sways and seductive interaction. Privacies surround us at all turns, on social media, in the news, in the paparazzi trends of the day – all vying for attention, often exaggerating, amplifying, or disregarding the question of the real altogether. And within this circulation of simulation and simulacrum, what matters is not the promise of truth but of – strange as it might seem to suggest – the promise of connectivity, maybe even the possibility of friendship.

## The Conspiracy of the Real

Reality is dead, says Jean Baudrillard, not because it has vanished but because of an excess – there is too much reality, too many realities, multiplied and conflicting and conjectured and imagined and staged and simulated. So many realities that the very idea of a reality principle has ceased to be meaningful in any significant way.

> Let us be clear about this: when we say that reality has disappeared, the point is not that it has disappeared physically, but that it has disappeared metaphysically. Reality continues to exist; it is its principle that is dead.[11]

But how is it that reality can continue to exist without a principle that makes it possible? That multiple realities can coexist means that despite appearances to the contrary, there is no longer a singular horizon of accountability through which reality might be seen or apprehended. That it seems otherwise – for Baudrillard – is more of a conspiracy than a relation, rendered and sustained by the ecosystem of technical ideology and virtual solutions. "The simulacrum is not that which hides the truth but that which hides the absence of truth."[12] And thus is born the post-truth era, out of the impossibility of any singular truth to which all lived realities can be held accountable. The conspiracy to end all conspiracies – what could be more insidious than to replace the very concept of reality itself with a technical construction called reality?

Now, I have always loved Baudrillard for his particular mode of succinct but ambiguous articulation, an observation that concepts reverse themselves when taken to extremes. His politics of philosophy work in service of a "production of vertigo."[13] Like intelligence: "When the hypothesis of intelligence ceases to be *sovereign* and becomes *dominant*, then it is the hypothesis of stupidity that becomes sovereign."[14] Like the real – rendered redundant by the proliferation of post-truth truths, requiring new modes of consent to be formed.[15] Like the image too – made ubiquitous to the point where all vision becomes accountable to the photograph. But it also strikes me that there is another version of this story, in which the disappearance of dominant modes of truth-saying and a scepticism towards the smooth and impenetrable logic of evidence-based argument, actually might serve as mechanisms for a different sort of world-building. For when the real is replaced by the real, the consequence is the counter-intuitive conclusion that realities can be replaced, not just by a technical double but by whatever idiosyncratic version of the story can be lived in a sustainable way. For I'm caught by the fact that – despite the disappearance of the real – I still wake up in the morning, autopilot my days, have some semblance of something that might be called experience, if not existence. And it's at that most mundane level of subjective living that I continue to find the highest stakes of Baudrillard's thought – the moment where instead of an argument to be believed, his ideas become a challenge to reconcile with the lived moment.

What is left is no longer the idea of truth but that of a sustainable (personal or collective) narrative – what matters is not the reality of the situation but the community that forms around it. For if we gamble against truth and reality – in their dominant and full-spectrum, technical forms – a strange sort of permission opens up to rethink the world, indeed to create the world differently. It might be called a simulacrum, but it is no less lived for the fact that it cannot be comprehensibly reduced to documentation and evidence. It is a gamble, but perhaps the only alternative to the smooth operations of technical logic is to install a double, a metaphysical secret agent that wagers itself not on evidence but on something else. Not intelligence in the modernist sense, where knowledge sets us free, but intelligence in the espionage sense, where knowledge can be deployed as leverage.[16] Not conspiracy but a form of conspiring, a post-simulation imagination that posts simulations precisely because to double the world at least opens it up to options, to differences, to alternatives. That they are not real is only a problem if one still believes in reality – that they might be imaginary is only a problem if one does not believe in the materiality of the imagination. Baudrillard calls it a "lucidity pact":

> What binds us to the real is a contract of reality. That is to say, a formal awareness of the rights and duties attaching to reality. But what we long for is a complicity and dual relation with beings and things – a pact, not a contract. Hence the temptation to condemn this contract – along with the social contract that ensues from it. Against the moral contract that binds us to reality we must set a pact of intelligence and lucidity.[17]

If Baudrillard's lucidity pact is to be taken seriously, what it amounts to is a purposeful attempt to live within the simulation – which is to say a gamble on the complexity of collectively formed and material living rather than an essentialist refusal of technological context. Thus, to Baudrillard's "lucidity pact" I would add an emphasis, on what he calls "complicity and dual relations," requiring that this pact be made not only with oneself but with others. Against inherited realities, a conspiring to re-make them differently. It is not an argument. It is a commitment – a pact or gamble coupled with an intent to hold ideological space and duration. Less a metaphysical proclamation and more a form of dwelling.

## Van Gogh's Right Ear

Baudrillard was a better philosopher than he was an artist, but there is one of his pictures that I always loved – *Sainte-Beuve* – an image of an old chair draped in red fabric that had clearly been inhabited in an extended way such as to leave an imprint of the body that occupied it.[18] In some ways it's a ghost story, but I think perhaps more importantly it's a picture of something ambiguous but still present because of, and despite, the vanished body. In this picture I see hope – that even within the lucid simulation of existence, marks are left, relationships made, impressions formed. For me, it's an image of dwelling, of space held and life lived and space occupied by bodies, changing or impressing upon the world around them in some way. And it makes me realize that even algorithms change through their interactions with me – customized as they are to receive many facets of input. Virtualities adapt in response to my patterns of inhabitation. That my actions in the world – real or not – might leave impressions of this sort is an interesting kind of thought. Without knowing whether there is any truth to the idea or not, I want to believe that this was Baudrillard's chair, and maybe that's why I like to dwell on it too – not exactly sitting on the chair but on the image, in a way that somehow sustains its inhabitation.

I'm stuck on the idea that dwelling is important because it seems to be all that is left when the world of appearances is reduced to post-truth simulation. Dwelling is also one of philosopher Johnny Golding's "eight technologies of otherness," which act as strategies for thinking otherwise in an age of prefabricated ideas and solutions – thinking against reason because reason no longer reasonably represents the complexity of lived nuance. She asks, "What if it were to be admitted that the usual, empty phrases – like to the so-called 'deep and violent cut' of meaning, truth, death, indeed identity itself: the 'who are we' and 'what are we to become' of science and of life – have collapsed under their own bloodless, sexless weight of self-reflective reason?"[19] Golding's critique is aimed at the generic construction of identity and the ways in which dominant ideologies foreclose on the possibilities of difference and otherness. For Golding, "self-reflective reason" is not the solution but part of the problem, and there is a "certain something" needed to negotiate the resulting terrain to expose the friction between selves and their self-reflective constitutions, lived realities that stand somehow against the total simulations of Baudrillard's virtual prophecies.[20] Her solution is to propose a different order of technology, not one anchored in digital systems at all but rather in "eight technologies which are themselves nothing more or less than relations, 'techniques,' or techné (in Foucault's sense): the everyday strategies we use, wittingly or no, to make all the we-selves into me-selves."[21] Conceptual markers of different ways to constitute meaning, Golding proposes curiosity, noise, cruelty, appetite, skin, nomadism, contamination, and dwelling as anchor points for thinking the materiality of self in an age of virtual, digital, and ideological simulacrum.

Dwelling for Golding is not a rigid concept but one that links concepts of home to those of attention, asking us to understand the stakes of thought for how it links place to care, commitment to comfort, and to the absolute uniqueness of the moment – suggesting dwelling as a way of thinking about inhabited time as a way of celebrating difference: "'difference' [as] something to be grasped, invented – that is to say inhabited – in all its glorious manifestations, productions, changes without refuse to a totalizing picture of reality."[22] But to inhabit differently is also to attend to difference in an attentive kind of way: to see differently, or in Golding's case, to hear differently. Less about seeing the picture and more about listening to what isn't there anymore. Golding suggests another metaphor of absence, not an inhabited chair but "Van Gogh's right ear" for situations like these, calling back to the story of the self-tormented artist who violently cut his ear in a desperate attempt to call out to the world.[23] In this story, Golding finds a form of phantom phenomenology that decries tools of technical apprehension in favour of other ways of empathizing with the world: "no lie (nor truth): only the radical geography of a fiction, continuous in all its dis-continuity."[24]

Yet something bothers me in this: an aversion to celebrating the pain of others. It is a space that is not mine to claim, unless it is first shared intentionally. But in an interesting twist, it turns out that Van Gogh actually cut his left ear, not his right – and the self-portrait that Golding meditates upon is a reflection painted by the artist looking at himself in a mirror. It's important because the painting makes it public, and Golding's reference to the "right ear" makes it clear that she is speaking about the ear of the painting – not the ear of the man. It may seem like a minor distinction, but for me it matters greatly. The representation gives permission to engage, to adopt the ear as metaphor – indeed to listen. This ear is one we are thus invited to put on (to inhabit, through his painting), listening in different ways, as a result. Following Golding, then, I put on Van Gogh's lost ear as if it were a mask or a filter for hearing (or exactly not-hearing) the world differently.

## Horseplay

The idea of dwelling on a painting or an image may not be the most intuitive line of thought, given that both visual forms share the pretence towards a directional bias that casts the viewer as a passive recipient of a finished object. Yet, the push against the status of finished objects is what sustains the stakes of engagement – otherwise there is no reason to engage. However, such a move away from a representational analysis of the image is, by necessity, to adopt a relational posture towards the camera, some form of dialogism or reciprocity that can acknowledge the beginnings of a new story being told. It is a political gesture in that it refuses pre-established truths or meanings and instead prioritizes relationships and context, subjectivities, ambiguities, with all the mess and vertigo such a repositioning entails.

In a beautiful essay on her personal relationship with a horse, Johnny Golding meditates on what it means to construct friendship across species boundaries, emphasizing that relationships of this sort are built on a form of engagement that unseats the dictates of logic and common sense in ways that – at times – can seem almost magical.[25] Friendship, for Golding, involves (among other criteria) a "certain kind of attunement, a certain kind of reaching out, a certain kind of response, a certain kind of respect, and a certain kind of play."[26] But most importantly, friendship cannot be made in isolation:[27] no more categorical differences (between human and animal, perhaps also between human and image) but a mode of engagement that plants itself firmly in the generative spaces of new kinds of story-telling, and thus new forms of truth-making, "to invent anew by supposing 'it could be otherwise' and then figuring out what and how this 'otherwise' might become real, alive, take root and flourish."[28]

Now I'm not sure that Golding would appreciate my desire to link her experience with Manhattan (the horse) to that of the camera, the tinfoil hat, or conspiracy, but I like to think that she would appreciate the spillage from conspiracy thinking to the idea of conspiring with others towards a different iteration of the future. At stake, for me, is the framework for building friendships, community, allegiances, which – erroneous or not – is generative of a certain possibility for realigning thought in relationship and response to the circulations of technical living. Conspiring together towards different forms of lived encounter.

But think about that in the context of photography. What if a photograph was a horse? It might be Trojan if that helps make it easier to imagine, but I actually think it's more powerful if it's actually just a horse – an actual horse that one might actually ride if – like Golding – one were able to build enough trust and reciprocity to make it viable to do so. It takes effort. And at stake is the idea of riding an image, of actually having to attune and adapt to a picture – perhaps by considering photography through the lens of animal studies, or indeed as an object of friendship, inflected deeply by the imaginary but accountable to the care that makes the relationship matter.

> Friendship is neither a gift bestowed nor an object of contemplation. Quite the reverse, friendship entails an economy of logic and gift exchange built of a wholly different order, imbued with a certain kind of attunement (listening), a certain kind of reaching out (event), a certain kind of response (-ability), a certain kind of respect (fullness), and a certain kind of play (-time), all diffractively generated without a single string attached. It is strictly born from the senses, and more than that, from a kind of exquisite, erotic, inhabited logic of the senses … It [friendship] only exists as an entangled encounter of embodied exchange.[29]

No first-causes; just awkward coexistences until some kind of common territory can be built. Golding calls it "horse-play,"[30] a kind of "superpositional empathy"[31] that "enables a certain mindfulness to emerge, one that sidesteps reason without being unreasonable, one that sidesteps logic without being illogical."[32] From this perspective photography is a muddy practice, not one tasked with clarifying the image of the world but of making more ambiguous the circulations of relational engagement.

## Conspiracy Thinking

Don't take my word for anything in this book – it could all be a conspiracy and I could be complicit in the circulation of an imaginary solution to the challenge of paradox in a digital age. But whether my word is good or not is not what is at stake since there is really nothing radical in words. Instead, it's the relationships that words are capable of forming that matter – that "radically matter" – as artefacts in a system of affective and post-truth circulation. "You tell the stories you need to believe," says novelist Rebecca Brown, and I think she's right.[33] Though, in the same breath, I ask myself what it means to say she's right and to realize that it's a story I need to believe. I like the idea that I might conspire with an image towards a different story than it might tell on the surface – not a didactic re-accounting of an inherited world but a collaborative re-telling of a future world apprehended in the blurry peripheries of vision. The kind of story that one can't see if one looks directly at it, but which manifests more presently when seen out of the corner of one's eyes, felt more than seen, intuited more than evidenced.

To adopt this stance is to give agency to the image – not as a static object distilled and displaced from time, but as a representative of a different sort of time, carrying with it a different kind of affect and intentionality. Not in service of the human project of technical documentation but something else – perhaps a rupture in the fabric of time, perhaps a shield or amplifier of a different imagination of the world, but in any case an active partner, foil, and catalyst with which I might choose to conspire.

To return to the exercise which began this chapter would be to note that Tinfoil Hats, as a participatory project, is a constructed photographic moment, but it is also a request to engage in a moment of self-reflective ambiguity – asking what stories we need (or want) to believe. Whether there are invisible signals blasting me from the sky is not what is at stake. It is more about posture – a question of whether I see room for myself to act as a co-conspirator of the futures being shaped and sustained around me. **Conspiracy thinking** is a creative strategy for post-truth community building. Such communities may tend towards ambiguity since they are not premised on deductive argumentation or clearly annotated lines of documentation. In such acts of conspiring, one moves away from the photograph as a marker of an historical moment and towards ambiguous new constellations of relational possibility. "The peculiar role of photography is not to illustrate the event, but to constitute an event in itself … to do so it must also remain in a sense a stranger to itself."[34] It's as easy as putting on a tinfoil hat.

# Postscript

**Exercise 7: Take a Picture of Yourself Imagining**

**Framing statement:** If someone told you that your fantasies were important, would you believe them or would you just think that fantasies are nice stories but ones that, ultimately, don't really matter in any substantial way? It's a rhetorical provocation, and a set-up for a rhetorical question: what are fantasies worth? Does it matter that we are able to imagine stories, fantasy narratives in which the rules of the real world don't really apply in the ways we're used to? And does it matter that some of these stories might even be impossible – not even remotely believable – except that insofar as they are stories, they begin to ask us for a strange form of belief nonetheless?

In the 1960s there was a story of the impossible – the story of a man who claimed he could project his imagination directly onto photographic film. His name was Ted Serios and among his advocates was the psychiatrist Jule Eisenbud who put Serios through a series of tests and experiments, designed to filter and channel and – ostensibly – prove the abilities that Serios claimed.[1] *Exercise in Psychic Photography* is an experimental project, loosely based on a recreation of experiments conducted by Serios and Eisenbud in which participants perform a simple experiment in thought-generated imagery. This is an exercising of the imagination and an act of holding space and time for the process of imagining one's relationship to the world of pictures.

**Guidelines:** This project holds purposeful space for what cannot be documented directly, asking participants to attempt to take a photograph directly of their mind. To participate, spend at least five minutes imagining something simple, attempting to hold – as clearly as possible – an image in your mind. Next, take a picture of your forehead while attempting to project the image from your mind directly into the camera. While it may be a task destined for failure, the premise of the project is that one never knows what might happen unless one tries. At the very least, your image will be one of the act of imagining, whether or not the imagination itself succeeds in finding its way to the camera. It requires an attitude of good faith.

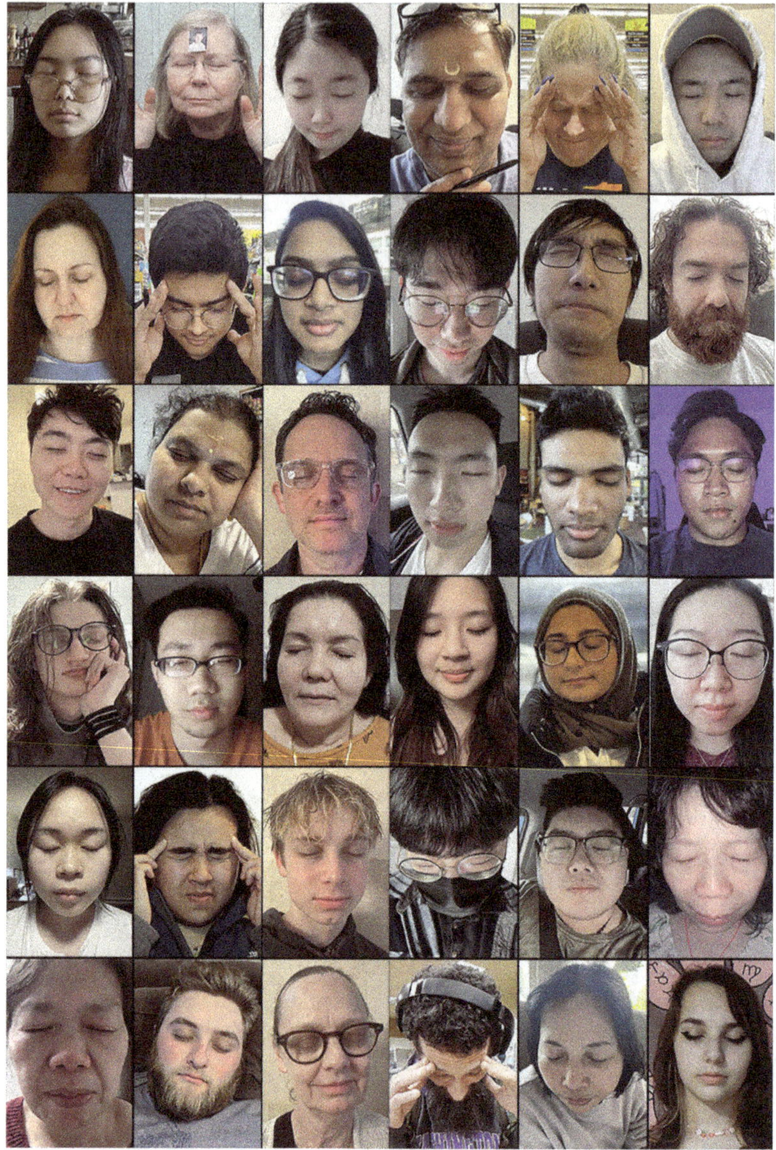

Figure 7.  Ted Hiebert, *Exercise in Psychic Photography*, compilation of participant portraits, photographs, 2022

## Exercise in Psychic Photography

I face a wall of faces, each one a tightly cropped portrait of a person. Some have their eyes closed as if caught in a moment of contemplation. Others stare at the camera – or through it – not really looking at me but instead looking with some other kind of difficult to place expression or intent. Each image distinct but brought together with a peculiar sort of commonality, an ambiguity, an event that seems nondescript but nonetheless present. Each image seems to be thinking or imagining – or at least I project onto the images that there is some other kind of projection in play in the minds of the people I witness, something that they are thinking or not thinking, something responsible for the commonality of contemplative form.

I will call this posture one of imagining, and I will say that it is clear to me that they are imagining something. Of course it is also entirely impossible for me to tell precisely what they are imagining. And perhaps that's the point – I can't tell what they are imagining, yet I can tell that something is happening that is not what I am seeing. Consequently I too have to imagine what they might be imagining, and in so doing I also begin to play in the game of imaginary exchange. I imagine what they might be imagining. I imagine that it might be funny to take a picture of myself as I imagine what it is that they are imagining too.

I have always loved the Ted Serios story for the challenge of thinking beyond the usual relationships between images and imagination. I have never cared if the images were real in a technical sense – though I suppose I would be disappointed to ever find out they were faked. What I love is the undecidability, and there is enough ambiguity in the story for me to sustain my attention. There is enough complexity too between the advocates and the sceptics, none of which really make fine enough arguments or demonstrations to build a case that stands the tests of conventional verification. The short version of the story is that Jule Eisenbud and many others believed Serios was actually psychic and had the ability to somehow project images from his mind directly onto film. He wouldn't be the first,[2] but he also didn't always get it right – the images were often blurry or only partially formed. They sometimes didn't turn out at all. They were inconsistent enough that they failed the scientific test of being repeatable and therefore verifiable. There were also inconsistencies in his process – he was often heavily inebriated and often used a small tube of cardboard that he called his "gizmo" to help focus his thoughts.[3] Most sceptics focus on the "gizmo" as the cheat in the process, arguing that Serios somehow smuggled images into the camera through the cardboard tube.[4] Again, however, none of the sceptics' attempted recreations of the process seem to match the originals – the tests of reproducibility again fail. The story remains one of ambiguous status but generative in its power to refuse proof or explanation or debunking. And so the Ted Serios story is one that must be thought in different ways, not as a test of the real but as a possible way of thinking differently about the configurations between minds and pictures.

My favourite set of images from the Serios archive is a set of images of his forehead. I think it's funny but also exactly what one might expect of a process that had him thinking at the camera and then taking a photograph – self-portraits of a psychic caught in the act of imagining. Perhaps he was imagining himself and caught himself on film; perhaps the camera did its proper job and captured him instead of his mind – whatever the case, it's in the psychic self-portraits that I find the truest distillation of the Serios project. For me, ambiguity is key. The story fails if one insists on reading it for the truth or falsity of the situation. Instead, the situation itself is what intrigues me, for its generative possibilities – whether those moments yield actual psychic photographs or failed images seems rather beside the point. What is the point is that he was there, imagining, and making the attempt to capture that act of imagination for the camera – in whatever ways he could.

## Ghost Images

Hervé Guibert's book *Ghost Image* opens with a beautiful story about a failed photo session in which Guibert strove to take an intimate portrait of his mother. As the story goes, his mother was tightly constrained in her fashion choices and demeanour by an overbearing husband (Guibert's father) who rarely let her decide her own appearance in the world.[5] Guibert's photo session, by contrast, sought to give all possibilities of appearance back to his mother, inviting her to pick her own clothes, make-up, poses, and expressions in a way that could serve to make visible some of the hidden complexity and nuance of the woman herself. In Guibert's account, the session was a tremendous success, a cathartic and deeply bonding experience shared by mother and son. Excited to see the results of the photo shoot, Guibert went quickly to develop the pictures only to find that the entire roll of film was blank, lost to a technical error of the camera that for whatever reason failed to capture the images and the event they had worked so hard to create.

It was, on one hand, a deeply tragic moment of failed documentation – but Guibert quickly realized that it consequently also became something else: the camera's refusal strangely amplified the incommensurability of their shared moment of experience. In some ways, the images were rendered more forcibly in their minds precisely because they failed to register on film – the singular archive of an intentional moment that persisted with such power precisely because it was lost to the technical gaze and perpetuated only their memory and their imaginations of what the moment was and could have been. The moment was theirs alone, unmarked by documentation yet firmly implanted in their minds as a result of a shared technical failure. Guibert called it a "ghost image" – a picture more powerful than any visual artefact because it belonged to the status of haunting rather than that of documentation.[6]

But what if all photographs were thought of in this way – not for the ways a picture reduces a lived moment to its representation but instead as a marker of precisely that which the camera can never see? It could be called imaginary, but it should not be dismissed on these grounds when the imagination has the capacity to create living ghosts in the form of moments remembered. Every photograph may be a tombstone of a moment, but if tombstones replace our memories of the lives they mark, then the loss is ours. And instead of thinking reductively about the image – or indeed instead of placing memory and technical images in a locked power struggle with each other – what if we took the opposite strategy? That is, what if we thought of images as ghost makers, precisely as markers of moments haunted by technical interruption but never reducible to a representative analysis.

Images as markers of – indeed in many cases generative of – the haunted world of lived encounter.

## Photographing Ambiguity

The true power of the camera is not to capture an image on film or on screen but to solidify a memory of a moment – or an idea – in the human mind. The difference between the two is most pronounced when the camera fails – leaving us with haunted memories that somehow refused the technical imperative to appear as visual images. But sometimes cameras can be made to fail on purpose, setting impossible tasks that would be spectacular if realized but whose point isn't really to succeed but to entertain the plausibility of a reshaped relationship with the lens. And sometimes success can be mitigated by slowing down the process of photographic capture – working against the tendency towards instant gratification by instituting a creative tangent, a challenge, a game. The results are pictures that precisely would not have existed without the camera itself – and moments too. And to engage in these experiments with others is to create dialogues that would not have otherwise existed, potential communities united by engagement with strange propositions. Connected by images.

After all the pictures have been taken, and the world reproduced an infinite number of times in images of all sorts, what remains is the game of using the camera to create new experiences or situations or conversations, and in so doing extend and resist the full-spectrum capture of a technical real. That's psychic photography – the Ted Serios story is perhaps the most romantic of artist dreams, capturing the unfiltered image of the imagination itself. But the picture isn't really the point. The camera is an alibi – an excuse to construct a different world or situation for the sake of the document, and in so doing, demonstrate the ways that different worlds and situations can be constructed.

*Exercise in Psychic Photography* is a production of ghost images.

Photographing ambiguity is an exercise in psychic photography.

# Notes

## Introduction

1 Jean Baudrillard, *Why Hasn't Everything Already Disappeared*, translated by Chris Turner (London: Seagull Books, 2009), 50.
2 Arthur Kroker, *The Will to Technology and the Culture of Nihilism: Heidegger, Nietzsche, Marx* (Toronto: University of Toronto Press, 2004), https://doi.org/10.3138/9781442620933.
3 See Karen Barad, *Meeting the Universe Halfway: Quantum Physics and the Entanglement of Matter and Meaning* (Durham, NC: Duke University Press, 2007), https://doi.org/10.2307/j.ctv12101zq.
4 See Donna J. Haraway, *Staying with the Trouble: Making Kin in the Chthulucene* (Durham, NC: Duke University Press, 2016), https://doi.org/10.2307/j.ctv11cw25q.
5 See Joanna Zylinska, *Nonhuman Photography* (Cambridge, MA: MIT Press, 2017), https://doi.org/10.7551/mitpress/10938.001.0001.
6 The idea of a reflective engagement is intended as a contrast to the idea of critique that was prevalent in art schools of the late twentieth century. Instead of analysis, I employ speculative and reflective strategies that jump off from the image and attempt to catalyse main themes gleaned from spending time with the picture. The intention here is to push against critique in ways often suggested in anti-racist and decolonial literature, eschewing assessment in favour of appreciative engagement. For an excellent critique of the critique model, see Felicia Rose Chavez, *The Anti-Racist Writing Workshop: How to Decolonize the Creative Writing Classroom* (Chicago: Haymarket Books, 2021).

7 The contact sheet might no longer be an object of common knowledge – the terrain of photography shifting as it has from darkroom practices to the digital. A contact sheet is a print made directly from a roll of photographic negatives. One page shows very small (film-scale) images of each negative on the roll of film, thus allowing photographers to see all their pictures from a single session in a condensed and easily referenced way. The digital equivalent would be thumbnails.

8 Serena Kataoka, "Feeling with Your Eyes: Petroculture and *Ice Follies*," in *Plastic Blue Marble – Catalyst: Amanda Boetzkes*, edited by Ted Hiebert (Seattle: Noxious Sector Press, 2016), 101–2.

9 See Amanda Boetzkes, *The Ethics of Earth Art* (Minneapolis: University of Minnesota Press, 2010), https://doi.org/10.5749/minnesota/9780816665884 .001.0001, and Amanda Boetzkes, *Plastic Capitalism: Contemporary Art and the Drive to Waste* (Cambridge, MA: MIT Press, 2019), https://doi.org/10.7551 /mitpress/11972.001.0001.

10 Amanda Boetzkes, "Ecologicity, Vision and the Neurological System," in *Art in the Anthropocene: Encounters among Politics, Aesthetics, Environments and Epistemologies*, edited by Heather Davis and Etienne Turpin (Ann Arbor, MI: Open Humanities Press, 2015), 276.

11 See Paul Virilio, *The Vision Machine*, translated by Julie Rose (Indianapolis: Indiana University Press, 1994).

12 Stendhal, *The Red and the Black*, translated by Roger Gard (London: Penguin, 2002), 374.

13 Joyelle McSweeney, *The Necropastoral: Poetry, Media, Occults* (Ann Arbor: University of Michigan Press, 2015), 6, https://doi.org/10.3998/mpub.7573327.

14 Peter Sloterdijk, *Critique of Cynical Reason*, translated by Michel Eldred (Minneapolis: University of Minnesota Press, 1988), xxxiii.

15 McSweeney, *The Necropastoral*, 3.

16 Margret Grebowicz, *The National Park to Come* (Stanford, CA: Stanford Briefs, 2015), 31, https://doi.org/10.1515/9780804793421.

17 Roland Barthes, *Camera Lucida: Reflections on Photography*, translated by Richard Howard (New York: Hill and Wang, 1981), 31.

18 Grebowicz, *The National Park to Come*, 61.

19 Éric Chevillard, *On the Ceiling*, translated by Jordan Stump (Lincoln: University of Nebraska Press, 2000).

20 micha cárdenas, *The Transreal: Political Aesthetics of Crossing Realities* (New York: Atropos Press, 2011).

21 cárdenas, *The Transreal*, 31.

22 See François Laruelle, *The Non-Philosophy Project*, edited by Gabriel Alkon and Boris Gunjevic (New York: Telos Press, 2012).

23 François Laruelle, *The Concept of Non-Photography*, translated by Robin Mackay (London: Urbanomic, 2011).

24 Vilém Flusser, *Towards a Philosophy of Photography* (London: Reaktion Books, 2000), 78.

25 See Katherine Behar, ed., *Object-Oriented Feminism* (Minneapolis: University of Minnesota Press, 2016).

26 Katherine Behar, *Bigger than You: Big Data and Obesity* (Goleta, CA: Punctum Books, 2016), 2.

27 Julian Huxley, "The Tissue-Culture King," *Amazing Stories* 2, no. 5 (1927): 451–9. https://archive.org/details/Amazing_Stories_v02n05_1927-08_017 /page/n1/mode/2up.

28 Jean Baudrillard, *The Intelligence of Evil or the Lucidity Pact*, translated by Christ Turner (New York: Berg, 2005), 17, 27.

29 Johnny Golding, "The Courage to Matter," in *Data Loam: Sometimes Hard, Usually Soft: The Future of Knowledge Systems*, edited by Johnny Golding, Martin Reinhardt, and Mattia Paganelli (Berlin: De Gruyter, 2021), 452, https://doi.org/10.1515/9783110697841.

30 Jule Eisenbud, *The World of Ted Serios: Thoughtographic Studies of an Extraordinary Mind* (Jefferson, NC: McFarland, 1989).

31 Joseph Beuys, as cited in Laurie Rojas, "'Beuys' Concept of Social Sculpture and Relational Art Practices Today," *Chicago Art Magazine*, 29 November 2010, archived 3 August 2020, at the Wayback Machine, https:// web.archive.org/web/20200803212507/http://chicagoartmagazine .com/2010/11/beuys%E2%80%99-concept-of-social-sculpture-and -relational-art-practices-today/.

## 1. Ecopoetics of Blur

1 Carlos Castaneda, *A Journey to Ixtlan: The Lessons of Don Juan* (New York: Simon and Schuster, 1972), 72.

2 Serena Kataoka, "Feeling with Your Eyes: Petroculture and *Ice Follies*," in *Plastic Blue Marble – Catalyst: Amanda Boetzkes*, edited by Ted Hiebert (Seattle: Noxious Sector Press, 2016), 101–2.

3 Donna Haraway, "We Have Never Been Human," a lecture at the Pacific Centre for Technology and Culture, University of Victoria, 18 March 2004, https://hdl.handle.net/1828/6848.

4 Donna Haraway, *The Companion Species Manifesto: Dogs, People, and Significant Otherness* (Chicago: Prickly Paradigm Press, 2003).

5 Donna J. Haraway, *Staying with the Trouble: Making Kin in the Chthulucene* (Durham, NC: Duke University Press, 2016), https://doi.org/10.2307 /j.ctv11cw25q.

6 Amanda Boetzkes, "Ecologicity, Vision, and the Neurological System," in *Art in the Anthropocene: Encounters among Politics, Aesthetics, Environments and Epistemologies*, edited by Heather Davis and Etienne Turpin (Ann Arbor, MI: Open Humanities Press, 2015), 276.

7 See Paul Virilio, *Politics of the Very Worst*, translated by Michael Cavaliere (New York: Semiotext(e), 1999), 81.

8 Amanda Boetzkes, *The Ethics of Earth Art* (Minneapolis: University of Minnesota Press, 2010), 182, https://doi.org/10.5749/minnesota /9780816665884.001.0001.

9 Paul Virilio, *Art & Fear*, translated by Julie Rose (London: Continuum, 2003).

10 Virilio, *Politics of the Very Worst*, 54.

11 Virilio, *Politics of the Very Worst*, 86.
12 Paul Virilio, *The Information Bomb*, translated by Christ Turner (London: Verso, 2000), 57.
13 Virilio, *Art & Fear*, 27–35.
14 Virilio, *Art & Fear*, 71.
15 Paul Virilio, *The Vision Machine*, translated by Julie Rose (Indianapolis: Indiana University Press, 1994), 72–3.
16 Virilio, *Politics of the Very Worst*, 89.
17 Virilio, *Politics of the Very Worst*, 101.
18 Birds Aren't Real website, https://birdsarentreal.com/.
19 Boetzkes, "Ecologicity, Vision, and the Neurological System," 276.
20 Boetzkes, *Ethics of Earth Art*, 178.
21 Boetzkes, *Ethics of Earth Art*.
22 Boetzkes, *Ethics of Earth Art*, 39.
23 Boetzkes, *Ethics of Earth Art*, 4.
24 Amanda Boetzkes, "Interpretation and the Affordance of Things," in *Heidegger and the Work of Art History*, edited by Amanda Boetzkes and Aron Vinegar (Burlington, VT: Ashgate Press, 2014), 272.
25 Virilio, *Politics of the Very Worst*, 89.
26 Amanda Boetzkes, *Plastic Capitalism: Contemporary Art and the Drive to Waste* (Cambridge, MA: MIT Press, 2019), 26, https://doi.org/10.7551/mitpress/11972.001.0001.
27 Boetzkes, *Plastic Capitalism*.
28 Boetzkes, *Plastic Capitalism*, 240.
29 See Jacques Lacan, "The Mirror Stage as Formative of the Function of the I as Revealed in Psychoanalytic Experience," in *The Blackwell Reader in Contemporary Social Theory*, edited by A. Elliott (Oxford: Blackwell Publishers, 1999), 61–6.
30 Boetzkes, *Plastic Capitalism*, 242.
31 Boetzkes, *Plastic Capitalism*, 240.
32 Boetzkes, *Plastic Capitalism*, 242.

## 2. Necro-Reflectivity

1 Stendhal, *The Red and the Black*, translated by Roger Gard (London: Penguin, 2002), 374.
2 See Jacques Lacan, "The Mirror Stage as Formative of the Function of the I as Revealed in Psychoanalytic Experience," in *The Blackwell Reader in Contemporary Social Theory*, edited by Anthony Elliott (Oxford: Blackwell Publishers, 1999), 61–6.
3 Guy Debord, *Society of the Spectacle* (Berkeley: Bureau of Public Secrets, 2014), 92.
4 Joyelle McSweeney, *The Necropastoral: Poetry, Media, Occults* (Ann Arbor: University of Michigan Press, 2015), 3, https://doi.org/10.3998/mpub.7573327.
5 Peter Sloterdijk, *Critique of Cynical Reason*, translated by Michel Eldred (Minneapolis: University of Minnesota Press, 1988), xxxiii.

6 McSweeney, *The Necropastoral*, 19.

7 McSweeney, *The Necropastoral*, 3.

8 Sloterdijk, *Critique of Cynical Reason*, 101.

9 Sloterdijk, *Critique of Cynical Reason*, xxxiii.

10 Sloterdijk, *Critique of Cynical Reason*, 101.

11 See Donna J. Haraway, *Staying with the Trouble: Making Kin in the Chthulucene* (Durham, NC: Duke University Press, 2016), https://doi.org/10.2307/j.ctv11cw25q.

12 Sloterdijk, *Critique of Cynical Reason*, xxxiii.

13 Sloterdijk, *Critique of Cynical Reason*, 101.

14 Peter Sloterdijk, *Neither Sun nor Death* (New York: Semiotext(e), 2011).

15 Albert Camus, *The Rebel: An Essay on Man in Revolt* (New York: Doubleday Books, 2012), 22.

16 Hahnemann, quoted in Sloterdijk, *Neither Sun nor Death*, 8.

17 Sloterdijk, *Neither Sun nor Death*, 8.

18 Peter Sloterdijk, *Thinker on Stage: Nietzsche's Materialism*, translated by Jamie Owen Daniel (Minneapolis: University of Minnesota Press, 1989), 15.

19 Sloterdijk, *Neither Sun nor Death*, 8.

20 Rolan Barthes, *Camera Lucida: Reflections on Photography*, translated by Richard Howard (New York: Hill and Wang, 1981), 31.

21 See Arthur Kroker, *The Will to Technology and the Culture of Nihilism* (Toronto: University of Toronto Press, 2004), https://doi.org/10.3138/9781442620933.

22 McSweeney, *The Necropastoral*, 41.

23 McSweeney, *The Necropastoral*, 42.

24 McSweeney, *The Necropastoral*, 77.

25 McSweeney, *The Necropastoral*, 177.

26 McSweeney, *The Necropastoral*.

27 Jean Baudrillard, *The Intelligence of Evil or the Lucidity Pact*, translated by Chris Turner (New York: Berg, 2005), 18.

28 In 1940 the Argentinian writer Adolfo Bioy Casares wrote a novel titled *The Invention of Morel*, in which a fugitive was banished to a deserted island on which there was a machine that generated a total and immersive simulation of the environment, including a community of people going about a set of recorded tasks. The challenge the protagonist faced was not to dispel the simulation but to find ways to authentically integrate himself within its workings. See Adolfo Bioy Casares, *The Invention of Morel*, translated by Ruth Simms (New York: New York Review Books, 2003).

29 McSweeney, *The Necropastoral*, 178.

30 McSweeney, *The Necropastoral*, 14.

31 McSweeney, *The Necropastoral*, 180.

## 3. Smash Metaphysics

1 Duchamp's most famous example of the readymade is probably *Fountain*, a ceramic urinal (1917) placed on its back and signed with the pseudonym R. Mutt.

2 Marcel Duchamp, "The Creative Act," in *Marcel Duchamp*, edited by Robert Lebel (New York: Paragraphic Books, 1959), 77–8.

3 Roland Barthes, *Camera Lucida: Reflections on Photography*, translated by Richard Howard (New York: Hill and Wang, 1981), 27.

4 Susan Sontag, *On Photography* (London: Picador, 2002), 10.

5 Ariella Azoulay, *The Civil Contract of Photography* (New York: Zone Books, 2008), 10, 13.

6 Margret Grebowicz, *The National Park to Come* (Stanford, CA: Stanford Briefs, 2015), 23, 61, https://doi.org/10.1515/9780804793421.

7 Barthes, *Camera Lucida*, 31.

8 Margret Grebowicz, *Whale Song* (New York: Bloomsbury, 2017), 112, https://doi.org/10.5040/9781501329289.

9 Grebowicz, *The National Park to Come*, 66.

10 See Roland Barthes, "The Death of the Author," in *Image-Music-Text*, translated by Stephen Heath (London: Fontana, 1977), 142–8.

11 Barthes, *Camera Lucida*, 31.

12 Barthes, *Camera Lucida*, 70.

13 Grebowicz, *The National Park to Come*, 31.

14 Barthes, *Camera Lucida*, 73.

15 Réné Magritte, *The Treachery of Images*, 1929, oil on canvas, 23.75 in × 31.94 in (60.33 cm × 81.12 cm), Los Angeles County Museum of Art, https://collections.lacma.org/node/239578.

16 Barthes, *Camera Lucida*, 89.

17 Barthes, *Camera Lucida*, 57.

18 Barthes, *Camera Lucida*, 53.

19 Barthes, *Camera Lucida*, 91.

20 It wasn't always this way. The shift, I learned by looking at pictures online, happened in 1987 (earlier than I might have imagined); finish line images from 1985 still show the work "FINISH" written to face the runners themselves. Perhaps, then, 1987 marks the year in which the race finished ahead of the runners – an endtimes imagination of the event itself.

21 Grebowicz, *The National Park to Come*, 23, 61.

22 Grebowicz, *The National Park to Come*, 61.

23 Grebowicz, *The National Park to Come*, 9.

24 Grebowicz, *The National Park to Come*, 31.

25 Grebowicz, *Whale Song*, 29.

26 Grebowicz, *Whale Song*, 99.

27 Grebowicz, *Whale Song*.

28 Grebowicz, *Whale Song*, 100.

29 Steven Shaviro, *The Universe of Things: On Speculative Realism* (Minneapolis: University of Minnesota Press, 2014), 61, https://doi.org/10.5749/minnesota/9780816689248.001.0001.

30 Grebowicz, *Whale Song*, 25.

31 Grebowicz, *Whale Song*, 100.

32 Grebowicz, *Whale Song*, 112.

33 Barthes, *Camera Lucida*, 6.

## 4. Non-Choreography

1 Éric Chevillard, *On the Ceiling*, translated by Jordan Stump (Lincoln: University of Nebraska Press, 2000).
2 Chevillard, *On the Ceiling*, 5.
3 See, for instance, Marshall McLuhan, *Understanding Media: Extensions of Man* (New York: McGraw-Hill, 1964).
4 Robert Bruce, *Astral Dynamics: A New Approach to Out-of-Body Experiences* (Newburyport, MA: Hampton Roads, 1999).
5 micha cárdenas, *The Transreal: Political Aesthetics of Crossing Realities* (New York: Atropos Press, 2011), 23.
6 cárdenas, *The Transreal*, 35.
7 See François Laruelle, *The Non-Philosophy Project*, edited by Gabriel Alkon and Boris Gunjevic (New York: Telos Press, 2012).
8 François Laruelle, *The Concept of Non-Photography*, translated by Robin Mackay (London: Urbanomic, 2011), 39.
9 cárdenas, *The Transreal*, 24.
10 Laruelle, *The Concept of Non-Photography*, 2–3.
11 Laruelle, *The Non-Philosophy Project*, 207.
12 Karen Barad's discussion of superposition and quantum entanglement as social metaphors is well known and permeates her text, *Meeting the Universe Halfway: Quantum Physics and the Entanglement of Matter and Meaning* (Durham, NC: Duke University Press, 2007), https://doi.org/10.2307/j.ctv12101zq. For Laruelle's reference to superposition and other quantum principles see *The Concept of Non-Photography*, viii.
13 Jean Baudrillard, *The Intelligence of Evil or the Lucidity Pact*, translated by Christ Turner (New York: Berg, 2005), 40.
14 Baudrillard, *The Intelligence of Evil*, 27.
15 Laruelle, *The Concept of Non-Photography*, 1–6.
16 Laruelle, *The Concept of Non-Photography*, 3.
17 Laruelle, *The Concept of Non-Photography*, viii.
18 Laruelle, *The Non-Philosophy Project*, 207.
19 Pataphysics is an invention of the French playwright Alfred Jarry, who defined it as a "science of imaginary solutions" and as a study of the "laws governing exception." See Alfred Jarry, *Exploits and Opinions of Dr. Faustroll, Pataphysician*, translated by Simon Watson Taylor (Boston: Exact Change, 1996).
20 François Laruelle, *Photo-Fiction, a Non-Standard Aesthetics*, translated by Drew S. Burk (Minneapolis: Univocal, 2012), 6, 17, 42, 59.
21 John Ó Maoilearca, *All Thoughts Are Equal: Laruelle and Nonhuman Philosophy* (Minneapolis: University of Minnesota Press, 2015), 263, https://doi.org/10.5749/minnesota/9780816697342.001.0001.
22 College of "Pataphysics," in *101 Words of Pataphysics*, translated by Ted Hiebert and Alastair Brotchie (Seattle: Noxious Sector Press, 2019), 88–90.
23 Ó Maoilearca, *All Thoughts Are Equal*, 25.
24 Laruelle, *The Concept of Non-Photography*, 10.
25 Laruelle, *The Non-Philosophy Project*, 219.

26 cárdenas, *The Transreal*, 28.

27 cárdenas, *The Transreal*, 24.

28 cárdenas, *The Transreal*, 35.

29 cárdenas, *The Transreal*, 23.

30 cárdenas, *The Transreal*, 43.

31 For more on *Becoming Dragon*, see the artist's website: micha cárdenas, "Becoming Dragon," accessed 21 October 2024, https://michacardenas.sites.ucsc.edu/becoming-dragon/.

32 Laruelle, *The Non-Philosophy Project*, 219.

33 cárdenas, *The Transreal*, 38.

34 *Local Autonomy Networks (Autonets), 2012*, is an artivist project focused on creating networks of communication to increase community autonomy and reduce violence against women, LGBTQI people, people of colour, and other groups who continue to survive violence on a daily basis. More details can be found on the artist's website: micha cárdenas, "Autonets," accessed 21 October 2024, https://michacardenas.sites.ucsc.edu/autonets/.

35 The project is called *Unstoppable – DIY Bulletproof Clothing*, 2015, a collaboration among micha cárdenas, Patrisse Cullors, Edxie Betts, and Chris Head, which the artists describe as a set of materials and processes for producing DIY bulletproof clothing at low to no cost. UNSTOPPABLE is art as intervention. More details can be found on the artist's website: micha cárdenas, "Unstopable," accessed 21 October 2024, https://michacardenas.sites.ucsc.edu/unstoppable/.

36 *Sin Sol / No Sun* is an augmented reality game that allows users to experience the feelings of a climate change event in order to deeply consider how climate change disproportionately effects immigrants, trans people, and disabled people. Produced in collaboration with Marcelo Viana Neto, Adrian Phillips, Kara Stone, Abraham Avnisan, Wynne Greenwood, Morgan Thomas, and Dorothy Santos. More details can be found on the artist's website: https://michacárdenas.sites.ucsc.edu/sin-sol-no-sun/.

37 cárdenas, *The Transreal*, 64.

38 Laruelle, *The Concept of Non-Photography*, 6.

39 Martin Heidegger, *The Question Concerning Technology and Other Essays*, translated by William Lovitt (New York: Harper & Row, 1977), 4.

## 5. Digital Darkness

1 Vilém Flusser, *Towards a Philosophy of Photography* (London: Reaktion Books, 2000), 17.

2 At stake for Flusser is the question of human freedom. See Vilém Flusser, *Towards a Philosophy of Photography*, 80–2.

3 CV Dazzle is a project developed by artist Adam Harvey. Details on the CV Dazzle website: https://cvdazzle.com/.

4 CV Dazzle is a project developed by artist Adam Harvey. Details on the CV Dazzle website: https://cvdazzle.com/.

5 Flusser, *Towards a Philosophy of Photography*, 25.

6 Katherine Behar, *Bigger than You: Big Data and Obesity* (Goleta, CA: Punctum Books, 2016), 2.

7 Behar, *Bigger than You.*

8 Katherine Behar, ed., *Object-Oriented Feminism* (Minneapolis: University of Minnesota Press, 2016), 139.

9 Katherine Behar, "Artificial Ignorance," in *Chimeras: Inventory of Synthetic Cognition*, edited by Anna Engelhardt and Ilan Manouach (Athens: Onassis Publications, 2022), 61–5.

10 Flusser, *Towards a Philosophy of Photography*, 9.

11 Flusser, *Towards a Philosophy of Photography*, 27, 71.

12 The phrase "placebo ergo sum" comes from an earlier work in which I think about Lacan in the context of mirrors and self-delusion. See Ted Hiebert, "The Lacanian Conspiracy," *CTheory* 28, no. 2 (2005).

13 Flusser, *Towards a Philosophy of Photography*, 31.

14 Flusser, *Towards a Philosophy of Photography*, 25.

15 Flusser, *Towards a Philosophy of Photography*, 78.

16 Flusser, *Towards a Philosophy of Photography*, 9.

17 Flusser, *Towards a Philosophy of Photography*, 27, 71.

18 Flusser, *Towards a Philosophy of Photography*, 21.

19 Flusser, *Towards a Philosophy of Photography*, 10.

20 Adam D.I. Kramer, Jamie E. Guillory, and Jeffrey T. Hancock, "Experimental Evidence of Massive-Scale Emotional Contagion through Social Networks," *Proceedings of the National Academy of Sciences of the United States of America (PNAS)* 111, no. 24 (2 June 2014): 8788–90, https://doi.org/10.1073/pnas.1320040111.

21 Katherine Behar, "Post Haste: Communicative Capitalism, Context Collapse, and Decelerationist Aesthetics," a keynote lecture at *Tuning Speculation IV*, Toronto, 18 November 2016.

22 Behar, *Object-Oriented Feminism*, 9.

23 Behar, *Object-Oriented Feminism*, 5.

24 Behar, *Bigger than You*, 7.

25 Behar, *Object-Oriented Feminism*, 123.

26 Behar, *Object-Oriented Feminism*, 126.

27 Behar, *Object-Oriented Feminism*, 139.

28 Behar, *Object-Oriented Feminism.*

29 Behar, *Object-Oriented Feminism.*

30 Behar, *Bigger than You*, 43.

31 Behar, *Object-Oriented Feminism*, 138.

32 Behar, artist statement: Knock Knock, from the artist's website: Katherine Behar, "Knock Knock," 2019, accessed 21 October 2024, https://katherinebehar.com/art/knock-knock/index.html.

33 The technical details of this kind of encryption (SHA-256) are potentially relevant, since Alexa is not actually trying to guess a number but a verification code that would constitute a kind of handshake between the two devices, acknowledging that the number had been guessed without actually ever disclosing the number itself.

34 Behar, *Object-Oriented Feminism*, 124.
35 Behar, *Bigger than You*, 2.
36 Behar, *Bigger than You*, 2–3.

## 6. Conspiracy Thinking

1 Julian Huxley, "The Tissue-Culture King," *Amazing Stories* 2, no. 5 (1927): 451–9. https://archive.org/details/Amazing_Stories_v02n05_1927-08_017 /page/n1/mode/2up.
2 Ali Rahimi, Ben Recht, Jason Taylor, and Noah Vawter, "On the Effectiveness of Aluminum Foil Helmets: An Empirical Study," 17 February 2005, archived 22 February 2017, at the Wayback Machine, https://web .archive.org/web/20170222192434/https://keysduplicated.com/~ali /helmet/.
3 Rahimi et al., "On the Effectiveness of Aluminum Foil Helmets."
4 Jean Baudrillard, *Seduction*, translated by Brian Singer (London: Macmillan, 1990), 7.
5 Johnny Golding, "The Courage to Matter," in *Data Loam: Sometimes Hard, Usually Soft: The Future of Knowledge Systems*, edited by Johnny Golding, Martin Reinhardt, and Mattia Paganelli (Berlin: De Gruyter, 2021), 452, https://doi.org/10.1515/9783110697841-045.
6 Sue Golding, "A Word of Warning," in *The Eight Technologies of Otherness*, edited by Sue Golding (London: Routledge, 1997), xii–xiv.
7 Golding, "A Word of Warning," xiii.
8 Jean Baudrillard, *The Intelligence of Evil or the Lucidity Pact*, translated by Christ Turner (New York: Berg, 2005), 17, 27.
9 Baudrillard, *The Intelligence of Evil*, 87.
10 Golding, "A Word of Warning," xiii.
11 Baudrillard, *The Intelligence of Evil*, 18.
12 Baudrillard, *The Intelligence of Evil*, 32.
13 Baudrillard, *The Intelligence of Evil*, 215.
14 Baudrillard, *The Intelligence of Evil*, 179.
15 "When truth and reality were made to take lie-detector tests, they themselves confessed to not believing in truth and reality." Baudrillard, *The Intelligence of Evil*, 87.
16 Baudrillard, *The Intelligence of Evil*, 47–9.
17 Baudrillard, *The Intelligence of Evil*, 45–6.
18 Jean Baudrillard, *Sainte Beuve*, 1987. Giclée print on cotton paper, 90 × 60 cm.
19 Golding, "A Word of Warning," xii.
20 Golding, "A Word of Warning."
21 Golding, "A Word of Warning," xiii.
22 Johnny Golding, "Fractal Philosophy (and the Small Matter of Learning How to Listen): Attunement as the Task of Art," in *Code Drift: Essays in Digital Culture*, edited by Arthur Kroker and Marilouise Kroker, 20–51 (Victoria, BC: CTheory Books, 2010).
23 Golding, "Fractal Philosophy."

24 Sue Golding, "Curiosity," in *The Eight Technologies of Otherness*, edited by Sue Golding (London: Routledge, 1997), 23.

25 Johnny Golding, "Friendship," in *The Edinburgh Companion to Animal Studies*, edited by Lynn Turner, Undine Sellbach, and Ron Broglio (Edinburgh: Edinburgh University Press, 2018), 267.

26 Golding, "Friendship," 262.

27 Golding, "Friendship," 263.

28 Johnny Golding, *The 9th Technology of Otherness: A Certain Kind of Debt* (London: Royal College of Art Research Repository, 2013), 6.

29 Golding, "Friendship," 262.

30 Golding, "Friendship," 267.

31 Golding, "Friendship," 272.

32 Golding, "Friendship," 266–7.

33 See Rebecca Brown, *You Tell the Stories You Need to Believe* (Seattle: Chatwin Books, 2022), https://doi.org/10.3366/edinburgh/9780748638376.003.0009.

34 Baudrillard, *The Intelligence of Evil*, 99.

**Postscript**

1 Jule Eisenbud, *The World of Ted Serios: Thoughtographic Studies of an Extraordinary Mind* (Jefferson, NC: McFarland, 1989).

2 There have been other reported accounts of psychic photography at various historical moments. Some of the most prominent are claims by Japanese psychologist Tomokichi Fukurai (1910) and Russian psychic Uri Gellar (1995). Fukurai's experiments are especially interesting and accounted for in his book *Clairvoyance & Thoughtography* (London: Rider, 1931).

3 As described in Allison Meier, "The Man Who Tried to Photograph Thoughts," *Hyperallergic*, 4 December 2013, https://hyperallergic.com/96583/the-man-who-tried-to-photograph-thoughts/.

4 For instance, critic David Eisendrath, who discusses his theory in the Arthur C. Clark *World of Strange Powers* episode on Ted Serios, YouTube video, 9:21, https://www.youtube.com/watch?v=tsSWQzWKj6Y&t=310s.

5 Hervé Guibert, *Ghost Image*, translated by Robert Bononno (Chicago: University of Chicago Press, 1982), 11.

6 Guibert, *Ghost Image*, 16.

# Index

www.ingramcontent.com/pod-product-compliance
Lightning Source LLC
Jackson TN
JSHW060722140425
82217JS00008B/1